Sulcata Tortoise Pet (

The Captive Care of Sulcata Tortoises.

Sulcata Tortoise care, behavior, enclosures, feeding, health, costs, myths and interaction.

by

Ben Team

Table of Contents

About the Author

The author, Ben Team, is an environmental educator and author with over 16 years of professional reptile-keeping experience. Ben currently maintains www.FootstepsInTheForest.com, where he shares information, narration and observations of the natural world. When not writing about plants, animals and habitats, Ben enjoys spending time with his beautiful wife.

Foreword

Few animals are as fascinating as those that push the boundaries of size.

Whereas rodents, frogs and insects are more common in (and critical to) the world's habitats, it is the whales, giraffes and buffalo that capture the human imagination.

This is no revelation; nearly every industry in the world – from Hollywood to cereal manufacturers to conservation groups -- has used large creatures to help achieve their goals.

Simply put, big animals draw big crowds. However, some of these giants – namely, the reptiles – attract more than their share of the attention.

***

Despite the awe tigers, giant pandas and elephants evoke, these mammals remain familiar. We look into their eyes and see a similar gaze, returning our own.

Reptiles, by contrast, are alien creatures, whose bodies and lifestyles could scarcely be any different from our own. Instead of a thin covering of body hair, they bear scales or leathery skin; instead of maintaining consistent body temperatures, they warm up and cool down over the course of the day.

***

Large reptiles are always among the most popular animals at zoos and wildlife parks – there is never a shortage of people watching the crocodilians, Komodo dragons or anacondas.

Despite their popularity, many fear these animals – few onlookers would dare to enter their cages. However, not all large reptiles are predators; some, such as the giant tortoises, represent virtually no threat at all; they are as harmless as they are amazing.

It is this combination of exotic biology and a gentle demeanor, which makes giant tortoises among the most popular and beloved animals in the world.

***

African spurred tortoises (*Centrochelys* [*Geochelone*] *sulcata*) – colloquially called "sulcatas" --- are the third largest tortoise in the world, and the largest species native to a major continent.

Hailing from north-central Africa, sulcatas spend their lives feeding on grasses, succulents and flowers, while avoiding lions, humans and other predators. While they fail to reach the size of Galapagos (*Geochelone nigra*) and Aldabra tortoises (*Aldabrachelys gigantea*), they grow large enough to turn heads and capture the attention of all who spend time in their company.

As you may expect, many people desire to incorporate these amazing creatures into their lives. In the broadest terms, this is quite possible; sulcatas adapt well to captivity, and exhibit the same gentle personality that most of their relatives do.

However, a giant tortoise requires more resources and dedication than most would-be keepers are willing or able to provide, which leads to a frustrated human and a neglected tortoise – clearly an undesirable outcome.

Accordingly, it is of paramount importance to understand the nature of sulcata husbandry before deciding to embark upon the journey.

***

As sulcatas have become more popular among reptile enthusiasts, they have become more common in the marketplace. In fact, many would argue that they have become *too* available; most reptile expos, online merchants and retail pet stores sell adorable baby sulcatas.

This availability has increased the number of sulcatas purchased impulsively, which is obviously not a recipe for success. Within a few weeks, months or years, these keepers find that they are no longer willing or able to care for their pet, and are forced to find a new home for it (which is no small feat in itself).

Nevertheless, for a small percentage of reptile enthusiasts, sulcata maintenance is not a bad idea. In fact, for those with the space, resources and commitment necessary to provide their turtle with a high quality of life, few things are as rewarding as sharing your life with one of the world's largest tortoises.

***

If you believe you are well suited for a sulcata, it is your responsibility to learn as much as you can about these creatures *before* you acquire one. Wait to purchase your new pet until you have considered all aspects of sulcata ownership and come to terms with the notion of a life-long pet.

PART I: THE SULCATA TORTOISE

Properly caring for any animal requires an understanding of the species and its place in the natural world. This includes subjects as disparate as anatomy and ecology, diet and geography, and reproduction and physiology.

It is only by learning what your pet is, how it lives, what it does that you can achieve the primary goal of animal husbandry: Providing your pet with the highest quality of life possible.

Chapter 1: Sulcata Tortoise Description and Anatomy

While their size is somewhat atypical when compared to that of their smaller relatives, the basic morphology of sulcata tortoises resembles that of most other turtles.

They possess a typical, bilaterally symmetric vertebrate body plan, including a head, long neck, tail, four legs and a large shell.

Size

Hatchling sulcatas begin life as relatively small turtles, with carapace lengths of about 1.5 to 3 inches (3.8 to 7.6 centimeters) and weights of about 1 to 3.5 ounces (6 to 10 grams).

As adults, sulcatas are the largest terrestrial turtles to inhabit a continental landmass and the third largest terrestrial turtle in the world. Only the Aldabra giant tortoise (*Aldabrachelys gigantea*) of the Seychelles Islands and the Galapagos tortoises (*Chelonoidis nigra*) of their namesake Pacific archipelago outgrow sulcatas.

Most adults reach carapace lengths of about 18 to 24 inches (45 to 60 centimeters) and weigh between 70 and 100 pounds (30 to 45 kilograms). However, exceptionally large specimens may reach lengths of 36 inches (91 centimeters) and weights in excess of 150 pounds (68 kilograms).

Shell

The defining characteristic of sulcatas is their thick, heavy shell, which serves to protect them from the large predators of their native lands. When viewed from above, the shell has a distinctly oval shape.

Like those of all other living turtles, sulcata shells have a top (called the carapace), a bottom (called the plastron) and a portion of the shell that connects the two on the right and left sides, called lateral bridges.

The shells are derived from a combination of the rib cage and dermal plates (bony plates that originate within the skin). On top of the bone lie keratinized plates, called scutes.

Interestingly, the plate-like bones outnumber the keratin-based scutes. This means that the margins of the scutes do not occur in the same places that the bones fuse together. Likely, this arrangement makes the shell stronger.

Sulcatas have five vertebral scutes that form a row down the center of the back. Flanking the vertebral scutes are the coastal scutes, numbering eight in total (four on each side). Around the margin of the carapace lie 22 marginal scutes (11 on each side), and a single supracaudal scute, which sits right above the turtle's tail. Sulcatas have no nuchal scute (normally located directly above a turtle's head and neck along the anterior margin of the carapace).

The plastron and ventral scutes are visible on this young sulcata.

The plastron features six pairs of scutes, termed (moving posteriorly) the gulars, humerals, pectorals, abdominals, femorals and anals.

Turtles are firmly attached to their shells; they cannot crawl out of them, as is frequently seen in cartoons and comic strips. Accordingly, a turtle's shell grows along with the turtle.

At the time of hatching, sulcatas – like most other turtles – have relatively soft, flexible shells. The shell will harden over time, and this is no cause for concern.

The periodic nature of this phenomenon (the shells grow quickly during the active season and cease growing in the winter) causes growth rings to form on the scutes. These growth rings are particularly visible on sulcatas. However, contrary to popular perception, studies have shown that the growth rings are not a reliable indicator of an individual's age.

In some cases, turtles produce more than one growth ring per year; other turtles live in areas with very long growing seasons and short (or absent) dormant seasons, which disrupts the annual nature of the process. Additionally, the shells of many turtles – particularly mature specimens – show signs of wear. If this wear occurs near the growth rings, some of the rings may be obscured.

Sulcata legs are strong, thick and pillar-like in order to support their massive bodies.

Legs

To carry themselves through life while hoisting a robust shell, sulcatas require four strong, thick legs. Herpetologists refer to their legs as "elephantine," as they are structurally similar to the columnar legs of elephants.

Sulcatas possess five toes and claws on their front legs, while their rear legs only have four toes and claws. Their front legs are adorned with flattened, overlapping, armor-like scales while their rear legs are equipped with two or three large spurs (from which the species acquires one of its common names: the spur-thighed tortoise).

Head, Neck and Face

Like all other living turtles, sulcatas lack teeth. Instead, they have a bony beak (technically called a rhamphotheca), which is covered by a layer of keratin. Their beaks have evolved a sharp, cutting edge that helps them slice food into smaller pieces. The dorsal component of the beak is moderately hooked. The tongue is fleshy, muscular and used to manipulate food in the mouth.

The eyes of sulcatas sit on the sides of their heads, although the front of their faces are slightly constricted, which allows them to see in front of their face as well as to the sides. Their nostrils lie on the front of their faces, directly in front of their eyes.

Sulcatas lack external ears, but they possess internal ears. Their tympanum ("ear drum") lies under the large scales on the sides of their heads.

Tail

Sulcatas have relatively short tails. The tails play little to no role in locomotion or defense, but they do serve as the location for the vent, which is important in elimination and reproduction.

Although immature males and females have similar-looking tails, those of mature males are longer and thicker than those of mature females are.

Color and Pattern

Sulcata tortoises are typically clad in a combination of earth tones, ranging from yellow-brown to dark gray. Most specimens give the overall impression of a light brown or straw-colored tortoise.

The shell is characterized by a light-brown or khaki base color, interspersed with dark brown to gray markings that surround each scute. The skin color is usually darker than the base color of the shell, but the armored plates may appear yellow.

Sulcata coloration is most striking while the turtles are young; for the first few years of their lives, their colors contrast quite sharply with each other. Over time, their colors exhibit less contrast and become relatively uniform.

Occasional specimens display abnormal pigmentation.

Internal Anatomy

While the average turtle keeper need not understand the internal anatomy of their pet enough to perform exploratory surgery, a basic understanding of the turtle's internal world is necessary.

In most respects, turtles have internal anatomy that is similar to that of other vertebrates, such as humans. Accordingly, special attention is warranted for those aspects that differ from those of most other animals.

Skeletal System

One of the unique aspects of the internal anatomy of sulcatas turtles is their skeletal system.

As with most other vertebrates, turtles have both axial and appendicular skeletons. The skull, vertebral column and ribs form the axial skeleton, while the shoulder girdle, pelvic girdle and limbs comprise the appendicular skeleton.

However, in turtles, the ribs are fused to the shell. Unlike other vertebrates, whose pelvic and hip girdles are located *outside* the rib cage, turtles carry these bones *inside* their rib cage. While this helps to protect these areas from damage, this arrangement limits the mobility of most turtles.

Digestive System

The digestive system of sulcata tortoises is similar to that of other turtles, and, to a lesser extent, vertebrates in general.

Just inside the mouth likes the esophagus, which transports food to the stomach. From here, food passes through the small and then large intestines before being expelled from the vent.

The pancreas and spleen lie close to the stomach, while the gallbladder attaches to the liver, just as it does in most other vertebrates.

Circulatory and Pulmonary System

In general, the circulatory and pulmonary systems of turtles are similar to those of other reptiles.

Tortoises inhale and exhale through their mouth or nose, while the trachea carries air to and from two lungs. Because the turtle's shell is rigid, which prevents the ribs from moving (which would pump air into and out of the lungs), turtles have a collection of membranes and connective tissues that attach to the distal ends of the lungs. When these connective tissues contract and relax, the lungs empty and fill with air.

Like many other reptiles, turtles have three-chambered hearts, which feature two atria and a single ventricle. One atrium accepts oxygenated blood from the lungs, while the other atrium receives oxygen-poor blood from the body.

Both atria pump blood into a single ventricle, which then pumps the blood into the rest of the body. Normally, as in many other reptiles, this means that the turtle's body receives a combination of oxygen-rich and oxygen-poor blood. However, turtles have a primitive septum (wall) in their ventricle, which partially prevents the mixing of the two types of blood.

Accordingly, turtles have a slightly more efficient cardiovascular system than lizards and snakes do.

Urinary System

Sulcatas filter waste products from their bloodstream via their paired kidneys. They then store these waste products in the urinary bladder. These waste products are released in the form of uric acid, which requires relatively little water, instead of urea, which requires copious amounts of water.

Tortoises from arid regions, including sulcatas, often store water in their bladders. This helps them survive long droughts, as they can slowly withdraw the water as necessary. However, tortoises often release the contents of their bladders when frightened. While this may help repel a predator, the loss of water may cause them to become dehydrated in the future.

Turtles have a renal portal blood system, which means that the blood traveling through the rear half of the turtles' body is filtered by the kidneys before making it to the front half of the body. This has important implications in turtle medical care; medications cannot be injected into the rear half of the body, as they kidneys will filter the medications before they can circulate widely.

Reproductive System

Turtle fertilization occurs internally, so they must mate to reproduce.

Males have a single intromittent organ (penis), making them similar to crocodilians and birds, but very different from snakes and lizards, who possess paired reproductive organs (termed hemipenes).

The penis of male sulcatas is held inverted, inside the tail base. During mating attempts, the penis everts and protrudes outside of the vent.

Females have a pair of ovaries, in which eggs form and reside; and a pair of oviducts, which accept the eggs once they are released. The eggs join the sperm inside the oviducts, where they continue to develop.

Before the eggs are deposited, calcium and other minerals coat the surface of the developing embryos, thus giving rise to the eggshell.

Like females of many other species, sulcatas can retain sperm from a single mating for multiple years.

Chapter 2: Sulcata Tortoise Biology and Behavior

Sulcatas exhibit a number of biological and behavioral adaptations that allow them to survive in their natural habitats.

Growth

Like most other turtles, sulcatas grow rapidly while they are young; but their growth rate slows considerably once they reach maturity.

The growth rate of sulcatas varies widely from one specimen to the next, as well as in relation to the amount of food they can acquire. Captive sulcatas typically grow more quickly than wild specimens do – a 2002 study showed that captives often grow 1.4 to 2.6 times as rapidly as their wild counterparts do. (Ritz, Griebeler, Huber, & Clauss, 2010)

After hatching at lengths between 1.5 and 3 inches (3.8 to 7.6 centimeters), most individuals reach 5 to 7 inches (12.7 to 17.7 centimeters) in length and 2 pounds (907 grams) in weight by the end of their first year.

However, outliers occur on both sides of this average. Rare individuals may reach this size by six months of age while others may require two years to do so. By the third year of life, quick-growing individuals may reach 10 inches (25.4 centimeters) in length of more.

Specimens that reach exceptional sizes – such as some of the 30-inch-long (76-centimeter-long), 150-pound (68-kilogram) monsters seen from time to time – have invariably reached ages of 30, 40, 50 years or more.

Shedding

Like most other reptiles, sulcatas shed their skin; however, unlike snakes and lizards, who shed all of their scales at the same time, sulcatas shed on a rather continual basis. Because they replace very small pieces of skin at a time, the process is not terribly obvious.

However, at some times – particularly during periods of rapid growth – sulcatas may increase the amount of skin they shed in a short time period, which makes the process more conspicuous. Your pet may ingest his shed skin in an effort to avoid wasting any nutrients.

Sulcatas do not shed their scutes; instead, new material is added to the scutes during phases of rapid growth. The same scutes that adorn the top of a hatchling's carapace will be there for his 50th birthday, should he live that long.

Lifespan

Most turtles live long lives, and sulcatas are no exception. As is the case for most other chelonians, most mortality likely occurs among eggs, hatchlings and juveniles, rather than mature adults. Once they reach maturity, things like wildfires, disease and road mortality are likely the most significant threats; few predators (aside from humans) are capable of dealing with the robust shells of adult sulcatas.

Because of the difficulties involved in conducting very long-term research projects, scientists have accumulated relatively little research on the lifespans of wild-living tortoises. Nevertheless, the oldest documented captive sulcata was 54 years of age at the time of its death.

However, it is possible – perhaps even likely – that some individuals may live much longer than this. Suffice to say, with proper care, pet sulcatas should live for several decades, and possibly half a century or longer.

Senses and Intelligence

Sulcatas possess the same senses that most other turtles do. They have reasonably good eyesight, respond to tactile stimulation readily and appear to have a strong sense of smell. The sulcata's sense of hearing is average at best.

Turtles have a larger brain size index than most lizards and snakes do, but this does not mean they are especially intelligent. Nevertheless, sulcatas are able to anticipate husbandry protocols and feeding times. Many learn to associate their keeper with food, which can lead them to approach their keeper when entering the pen or nearing the cage. Some sulcata keepers describe the behavior as "begging".

Metabolism and Digestion

Sulcatas – like most other non-avian reptiles – have slow metabolisms. This not only means that it takes them longer than many other animals to process their food, but also, they require less food to remain alive. In general, ectothermic ("cold-blooded") animals require about one-fifth to one-twentieth of the food that similarly sized endothermic ("warm-blooded") animal do.

Sulcatas can go for long periods of time without food, and wild-living sulcatas consume much less food during the dry season than they do during the wet season. One of the limiting factors for their population density is likely the amount of food available in their habitats.

Locomotion

Despite their bulky build and ungainly appearance, sulcatas are capable of traveling long distances. Their strong, thick legs provide a stable base of support and their sense of balance keeps them from tipping over while walking.

If you watch a sulcata walk, you will usually see it move its legs in an alternating pattern. First, it swings the rear right leg and front left leg (for instance) forward, then, upon gaining purchase, it swings the other two legs forward. The front leg usually lands slightly before the rear leg does.

Of course, the animals adjust these movement patterns to negotiate uneven terrain or objects, so not all steps take on this pattern.

The head helps to maintain balance during locomotion, while the tail plays essentially no role.

Although they would never be considered good climbers, sulcatas often surprise their owners with their ability to scale obstacles. Sulcatas are also skilled at moving through the burrows they construct.

Diel Behavioral Patterns

Sulcatas are typically described as being diurnal, but in truth, they are most active during the early morning and late evening when temperatures are tolerable. In captivity, they will remain active during the day as long as conditions allow, although they may take naps during the middle of the day. Sulcatas are rarely active after dark.

Seasonal Behavioral Patterns

Unlike turtles from temperate lands, who must cease activity when temperatures fall during the winter, sulcatas live in the tropics and enjoy warm temperatures year-round.

However, while the temperatures of their native lands are warm all year, the amount of rainfall varies drastically from season to season.

The wet season (June through September) provides much more accommodating conditions than the dry season (October through May), which allows sulcatas to be more active during the wet season.

Some sulcatas may become dormant during the peak of the dry season – a behavior termed aestivation. During this time, the animals remain in long burrows to avoid desiccation. This is unlikely to occur in captivity, as long as you provide your sulcata with food and water at all times.

Defensive Strategies

When threatened, adult sulcatas withdraw their heads into their shell and use their armored front legs to help provide protection for their face. Combined with their considerable bulk, adults remain safe from just about every predator aside from humans.

Hatchling and juvenile sulcatas, on the other hand, are vulnerable to a wide variety of predators in their natural habitats. Accordingly, they usually try to remain hidden (or at least inconspicuous) as much as possible, in order to avoid attracting the attention of predators. When inactive, they will retreat to a burrow or hide amid dense vegetation.

Sulcatas are grazing animals, who will consume most grasses and weeds growing in their enclosure.

Foraging

Sulcatas primarily forage for food during the relatively cool morning and evening hours. Sulcatas are grazing animals, who consume a wide variety of grasses, flowers, forbs and succulent vegetation.

Sulcatas presumably locate most of their food visually, although their sense of smell may play a role as well. They may raise their heads high above the ground to help locate potential food sources, and they often appear to be attracted to bright colors.

Breeding Behavior

Adults usually begin breeding shortly after the wet season ends. During the process, males mount females from behind and insert their everted penises into the cloacas of the females. Males often emit vocalizations while breeding.

After successful mating and fertilization, the eggs begin developing inside the female's body. Nesting usually begins in the early summer, but it may occur later for populations in cool regions.

When the females are ready to deposit their eggs, they begin excavating a suitable nest. Sometimes, they may create several "test" nests before deciding which one they prefer. Females may urinate on the dirt several times during the process to facilitate easier digging.

After completing the nest and depositing her eggs, the female covers the nest; she will have no further contact with the young.

Hatchlings emerge from their eggs near the beginning of the next wet season, which gives them an extended period of time in which they can find food and grow before the first dry season occurs.

Male sulcatas are very territorial and engage in violent conflicts with each other. They often try to flip their adversary on his back, which can lead to the turtle's death if he is unable to right himself.

Chapter 3: Sulcata Tortoise Taxonomy and Phylogeny

Sulcatas were first described in 1779, and there is little doubt about their status as a species. However, scientists have shifted the location of sulcatas within the tree of life several times, as new data upended previous frameworks.

Reptiles in the Tree of Life

For decades, scientists have debated the definition of the term "reptile." (Anderson, 2003)

On the one hand, lizards, snakes, crocodiles and turtles are all instantly recognizable as reptiles, thanks to their scaly skin and other traits.

However, the reptile evolutionary lineage, when considered in its entirety, must also include dinosaurs, and their direct descendants, the birds.

Regardless of which definition taxonomists ultimately agree upon, the history of the group is relatively well known. Reptiles first evolved approximately 300 million years ago, when they branched off the amphibian family tree.

This lineage produced an amazing array of species, including dinosaurs, mosasaurs and pterodactyls, as well as the ancestors of modern snakes, lizards and turtles. Most of these lineages died out almost completely, but a few managed to survive to the present day. Currently, reptiles are represented by the following groups:

- Crocodilians
- Squamates (snakes and lizards)

- Sphenodontids (tuataras)
- Testudines (turtles)
- Birds

Testudines in the Tree of Life

All living turtles can trace their origin back to the same ancestral species, meaning that all living turtles are part of the same evolutionary lineage. Scientists call such groups monophyletic.

Two different names are commonly used to refer to the group, including "testudines" and "chelonians". While modern looking turtles likely appeared in the Jurassic period, a few primitive turtle fossils have been discovered from Triassic period deposits.

These turtles, which lived about 220 million years ago, differed greatly from modern turtles. Not only did they lack the proper shell of modern chelonians, they had teeth embedded in their upper and lower jaws.

Because of the unique body plan of testudines (a term that refers to all the various types of turtles, including marine, terrestrial and freshwater species), scientists have long debated the group's placement within the tree of life. Those swayed by morphological data believe that turtles are most closely aligned with Lepidosaurs (a group that includes snakes, lizards and tuataras). In part, this is based on the holes (fenestra) in the skulls of ancient turtles, which resemble those present in the skulls of lizards and snakes.

However, recent genetic studies of a wide variety of species has shed light on the placement of turtles within the tree of life, as well as the placement of individual species within the turtle umbrella. (Crawford, 2012)

According to this new research, turtles are the sister group to archosaurs (a group that includes crocodilians, birds and several extinct groups, such as non-avian dinosaurs). Lepidosaurs are the sister group to the ancestor of both archosaurs and testudines (a group named the archelosauria).

This means that the closest living relatives of turtles are crocodilians and birds, rather than snakes and lizards. Nevertheless, the two groups diverged from a common path hundreds of millions of years ago. So, while the two groups are each other's closest living relatives, they are not especially closely related.

As of October 2015, scientists currently recognize 341 living testudines, but this number fluctuates as new species are discovered, different species are synonymized and subspecies are elevated to the level of full species.

Sulcata Tortoises in the Tree of Life

Herpetologists categorize all living turtles in the order Testudines. The first major division in this lineage occurs between those turtles who withdraw their neck in a lateral plane (called the sub-order Pleurodira), and those who draw their neck back in a vertical plane, called the sub-order Cryptodira.

Like most other living turtles, sulcatas are members of the sub-order Cryptodira. In fact, all of the living tortoises are members of this sub-order, and they comprise the family Testudinidae.

Within the family, tortoises are grouped into any of several different genera. Sulcatas are members of the genus *Centrochelys*, and, although no other living members of the genus still walk the earth, at least five extinct forms have been described from the fossil record.

In recent decades, sulcatas were assigned to the genus *Geochelone*, so it is not uncommon to see them labeled as *Geochelone sulcata* in older works. In an effort to avoid confusion, some include the outdated genus in brackets when writing the species' scientific name: *Centrochelys* [*Geochelone*] *sulcata*.

Currently, scientists do not recognize any subspecies of the sulcata.

Chapter 4: The Environment of Sulcata Tortoises

Sulcatas are supremely adapted for their natural habitat, which is characterized by warm year-round temperatures, low annual rainfall and relatively little food.

Basic Geography

Sulcatas inhabit 10 different countries of north-central Africa, from Senegal and Mauritania on the west coast, through Mali, Niger, Nigeria, Chad, Sudan and South Sudan, to the east coast countries of Eritrea and Ethiopia.

This swath of land forms a habitat called the Sahel, which is a transitional zone between the Sahara Dessert to the north and the savannah habitat farther south. The Sahel is a flat, wide-open habitat that is largely covered in grasses, although scattered trees and patches of forest also dot the land.

Climate

Temperatures in the Sahel remain relatively high all year long. During the hottest months (those immediately preceding the rainy season), air temperatures may exceed 107 degrees Fahrenheit (107 degrees Celsius). However, maximum daytime temperatures are about 80 degrees Fahrenheit (27 degrees Celsius) in January, with nighttime temperatures dipping to about 50 degrees Fahrenheit (10 degrees Celsius). (Nicholson, 1995)

The northern portions of the Sahel average about 8 inches of rain annually, while the southern fringes of the habitat may experience as much as 24 inches of rain each year. Most of this rain occurs during the short wet season, between June and September.

Ecology

Sulcatas – like all other animals – do not live in a vacuum. They must live alongside countless other species, drawing resources from some and avoiding threats represented by others. Still other species play no appreciable role in the lives of sulcata tortoises.

Vegetation

As herbivores, sulcatas have an intimate relationship with the plant life of the Sahel. Unfortunately, few published studies of the animals' wild diet exist.

A variety of grasses, herbs and forbs grow throughout the Sahel. Some of the most common representatives include grasses of the genera *Aristida, Schoenefeldia, Cenchrus* and *Eragrostis*. Most of the region's grasses are annuals, although a few perennials also grow throughout the region.

Although trees are not widespread through the Sahel, they do grow in areas where the soil is sufficiently moist. Most of the region's native species are arid-adapted, which allows them to live in the seasonally dry area.

Acacia trees (*Acacia* spp.) are the most common woody plants in the region, but Baobab (*Adansonia digitata*) and Jujube trees (*Ziziphus mauritiana*) also grow throughout the Sahel. (Houerou, 1980)

In addition to the region's native plant life, agricultural crops are also grown in some portions of the Sahel. Some of the most commonly grown crops include millet (*Pennisetum typhoides*) and cowpea (*Vigna* spp.). Wild sulcatas will feed

34

on a variety of agricultural crops when the opportunity presents itself.

Predators

Relatively few large predators inhabit the Sahel. While the Sahel was historically home to predators such as lions (*Panthera leo*), wild dogs (*Lycaon pictus*) and cheetahs (*Acinonyx jubatus*), most of these have been extirpated over the last several decades.

Accordingly, the only large predators that represent a significant threat to mature sulcatas are humans. Nevertheless, Nile monitors (*Varanus niloticus*) and a variety of small mammalian carnivores live alongside sulcatas and likely predate on eggs and hatchlings when the opportunity arises.

Some of the larger birds of prey common to the region – particularly Egyptian vultures (*Neophron percnopterus percnopter*) who are known to drop stones on large eggs to crack them – may also prey upon hatchling sulcatas.

Other Associations

Occasionally sulcatas share burrows with other creatures -- particularly burrowing mammals. Hatchling sulcatas may preferentially use the burrows of other animals, as it is difficult for the tiny tortoises to construct their own burrow.

Sulcatas occasionally attract the attention of external parasites, primarily ticks. Some of these ticks can carry the bacterium *Cowdria ruminatium*, which causes Heartwater Disease among cud-chewing animals. Because of the potential for introducing the bacteria to North American ecosystems, the importation of wild-caught sulcata tortoises was prohibited in 2000.

Sulcatas can also suffer from a variety of internal parasites, including roundworms and flagellate protozoans.

PART II: SULCATA TORTOISE HUSBANDRY

Once equipped with a basic understanding of what sulcatas *are* (Chapter 1 and Chapter 3), where they *live* (Chapter 4), and what they *do* (Chapter 2) you can begin learning about their captive care.

Animal husbandry is an evolving pursuit. Keepers shift their strategies frequently as they incorporate new information and ideas into their husbandry paradigms.

There are few "right" or "wrong" answers, and what works in one situation may not work in another. Accordingly, you may find that different authorities present different, and sometimes conflicting, information regarding the care of these tortoises.

In all cases, you must strive to learn as much as you can about your pet and its natural habitat, so that you may provide it with the best quality of life possible.

Chapter 5: Sulcata Tortoises as Pets

Caring for any animal is a profound responsibility that requires both the means and the desire to provide it with a high quality of life.

It is imperative that potential keepers understand what is involved in caring for a sulcata tortoise, in order to make a deliberate, sober decision.

Sulcata Suitability

When provided with suitable housing, care and veterinary attention, sulcatas thrive in captive environments. The many sulcatas living happy and healthy lives in zoos, museums and educational institutions around the world demonstrate this clearly.

As long as the correct diet is provided, sulcatas are easy to feed, adapt well to the presence of their keepers and adapt to a wide variety of husbandry protocols.

Nevertheless, sulcatas are not appropriate for most keepers. While sulcata husbandry is relatively straight forward, they reach very large sizes, require expansive accommodations and have the potential for outliving their keepers.

While sulcatas are popular among many reptile enthusiasts, very few keepers are equipped to provide the proper care for them over multiple decades. However, experienced keepers, with the resources, desire and dedication befitting such amazing animals, can successfully maintain these tortoises in captivity.

Fortunately, most sulcatas available for purchase in North America and Europe are captive bred animals. Captive bred animals typically harbor fewer parasites than their wild-caught counterparts do and adjust better to captive life. Moreover, because captive bred sulcatas were not removed from the wild, they do not represent a threat to wild populations.

Sulcatas do suffer from a few common health problems, including a few that do not yet have definitive solutions. Accordingly, it is incredibly important for sulcata owners to continue to learn about their pets and work closely with their veterinarian.

What You'll Need

To keep a sulcata as a pet, you must provide it with all of its needs. This includes:

- A suitable enclosure
- Appropriate substrate
- Cage furniture
- Proper lighting fixtures and bulbs
- Heating equipment
- Monitoring equipment (thermometers, etc.)
- Food
- Husbandry tools (tongs, etc.)
- Transport containers
- Cage cleaning equipment and supplies

While every situation is different, a couple of fair scenarios are laid out in the following chart. These represent the initial costs of becoming a sulcata owner; they do not address on-going costs such as food and veterinary care.

Costs of Captivity

Inexpensive Option

Hatchling Sulcata	$50 (£32)
Large Plastic Storage Box	$50 (£32)
Lid Supplies and Hardware	$20 (£13)
Heat Lamp Fixture and Bulbs	$20 (£13)
Digital Indoor-Outdoor Thermometer	$15 (£9)
Infrared Thermometer	$35 (£22)
Cage Furniture	$20 (£13)
Food Dishes, Misc.	$25 (£16)
Total	$235 (£155)

Moderate Option

Yearling Sulcata	$100 (£65)
Large Pond Liner	$75 (£49)
Lid Supplies and Hardware	$25 (£16)
Heat Lamp Fixture and Bulbs	$20 (£13)
Digital Indoor-Outdoor Thermometer	$15 (£9)
Infrared Thermometer	$35 (£22)
Cage Furniture	$30 (£19)
Food Dishes, Misc.	$25 (£16)
Total	$825 (£539)

Premium Option

Adult Female Sulcata	$1,000 (£650)
Custom Enclosure	$1,000 (£650)
Digital Indoor-Outdoor Thermometer	$15 (£9)
Infrared Thermometer	$35 (£22)
Cage Furniture	$100 (£65)
Forceps, Misc.	$25 (£16)
Total	$2175 (£1436)

Myths and Misunderstandings

Before going further, it is important to distinguish between some of the myths and facts surrounding sulcatas and their care.

Myth: Sulcatas need friends or they will get lonely.

Fact: Sulcatas primarily live solitary lives in the wild; interactions are only common among breeding animals or combative males. Although some keepers house sulcatas in pairs or small groups for breeding purposes, they should usually be maintained singly in captivity to avoid problems with bullying. Even turtles that appear to coexist peacefully may be living in conflict.

Myth: Tortoises grow in proportion to the size of their cage and then stop.

Fact: Reptiles do no such thing. Most healthy tortoises continue to grow throughout their lives, although the rate of growth slows as they age. Placing them in a small cage in an attempt to stunt their growth is an **unthinkably cruel practice**, which is more likely to sicken or kill your pet than stunt its growth.

Myth: Sulcatas can survive on any vegetables you give them.

Fact: Diet is one of the most important components of sulcata husbandry and you must select food items very deliberately. Dietary problems often become quite serious before obvious symptoms appear and they can be very difficult – sometimes impossible – to rectify.

Myth: Reptiles have no emotions and do not suffer.

Fact: While turtles have very primitive brains, and do not have emotions comparable to those of higher mammals, they absolutely can suffer. Always treat reptiles with the same compassion you would offer a dog, cat or horse.

Myth: Sulcatas are tame animals and never hurt their keepers.

Fact: While sulcatas do not usually respond to perceived threats by biting, adults are massive animals that can cause minor injuries to careless keepers. Additionally, sulcatas are often eager eaters, who may mistake fingers and toes for food.

Myth: You can tell the age of a sulcata by counting the rings on its scutes.

Fact: While you can usually get a general idea of a sulcata's age by counting the rings on its scutes, the ring number rarely matches the age of the turtle precisely. At best, a ring count provides you with an estimate of the turtle's age.

Chapter 6: Your Sulcata's Enclosure

The first thing that you need to keep a sulcata as a pet is an enclosure – it is the defining characteristic of captivity!

Over the years, keepers have used a wide variety of enclosure types, each of which offers different benefits and drawbacks. Some keepers prefer inexpensive, functional enclosures and place a premium on things like cost, durability and ease of maintenance, while other keepers desire to build the most visually impressive habitat possible. Still others may design an enclosure well suited for captive reproduction.

Similarly, keepers differ on the space requirements of turtles; some find relatively modest cage sizes to be sufficient, while others prefer to provide their turtles with larger accommodations.

Regardless of which side of the spectrum you fall on, you must always provide your pet with an enclosure that is large enough to meet the turtle's basic needs – minimally including sufficient room to establish thermal gradients, permit exercise and allow mental stimulation for the animal.

As you proceed, consider all of the variables facing you and your pet, and design a habitat that best fits your circumstances.

Indoor or Outdoor?

The first major decision you must make with respect to the enclosure is its location. Specifically, you must decide whether you wish to keep your sulcata indoors or outdoors.

Both approaches have their merits and challenges, and you must decide which approach is best for your pet.

Because of their lightning needs, most tortoises thrive best when kept outdoors and allowed to bask in unfiltered, natural sunlight. While reptile lighting systems have come a long way in the last few decades, no lightbulb will ever be able to produce the same quality and intensity of light as the sun does.

Further, because sulcatas reach immense sizes, and few keepers have sufficient indoor space to accommodate such massive pets, most sulcata keepers have no other option besides outdoor maintenance.

This is obviously not possible in all locations (such as the northeastern United States or northern Europe), as sulcatas require warm, relatively dry conditions to thrive. Accordingly, it is often difficult to keep a sulcata as a pet, unless you live in an area conducive to outdoor housing.

However, even if the local climate is suitable for maintaining their health, outdoor housing is not without its drawbacks – particularly when dealing with small sulcatas.

Small sulcatas are at greater risk to predators and less tolerant of temperature extremes than the adults are. They are also more difficult to monitor in outdoor enclosures (unless the enclosures are very small), which presents additional challenges for the keeper.

Considering all the various factors, the best path forward – and the one embraced by most sulcata keepers – is to keep your sulcata indoors while it is young, and then move to an outdoor husbandry regimen, once it is large

enough to be safe from predators and better able to tolerate temperature extremes.

Sulcata Safety

While large individuals are safe from most predators (although rodents may gnaw on sleeping tortoises of any size), the list of potential suburban predators that may prey upon a small sulcata includes:

- Snakes
- Herons
- Raccoons
- Foxes
- Feral cats
- Feral dogs
- Coyotes
- Hawks
- Owls
- Minks
- Weasels
- Crows
- Ravens
- Opossums

Accordingly, it is imperative that you take steps to keep small individuals safe if you choose to house your tortoise outdoors.

Each of these predators relies on a different skill set to find and capture prey. This means that you may need to employ multiple safety features to protect your pet.

For example, a smooth wall 4 to 6 feet (1.2 to 1.8 meters) high surrounding the habitat will likely keep out most snakes and feral dogs, but it will do very little to keep out hawks, owls or crows. Conversely, a mesh cover with an open weave may prevent birds from dining on your turtle, but it will do little to keep out snakes.

Digging predators – dogs, weasels, foxes and others – also represent a tunneling threat; so, you must construct the wall so that it penetrates below ground level for a distance of at least 1 to 2 feet (30 to 60 centimeters).

While large sulcatas may be relatively safe from predators, determined humans may steal or harm your pet. Locks and security systems will reduce the chances of people accessing your pet, but they provide no guarantees.

Although they are not true "predators" in the strictest sense of the word, rodents may gnaw on sleeping tortoises of all sizes, so you must take all reasonable measures to exclude them from the habitat.

Design and Materials

Keeping turtles indoors requires the use of a large container of some sort. Plastic storage boxes, pond liners and cattle troughs, are a few of the most commonly used items, but virtually any smooth-sided, non-toxic, durable container will work. Commercial tubs built specifically for turtles and tortoises are also available.

If you live in a pet- and child-free home, you can forgo a lid for the cage, but if small creatures have access to the habitat, a lid is necessary.

Make the lid from metal mesh or screen, which will not only provide for adequate ventilation, it will allow your lights to illuminate and heat the cage.

If you prefer, you can use commercially built, plastic reptile caging for young tortoises, but, as your turtle will be too big for indoor maintenance within a few years, few find such cages cost effective. Additionally, many plastic reptile cages lack sufficient ventilation for sulcatas.

Aquariums and cages with glass doors are not appropriate for sulcatas. Unfamiliar with the principle of transparent materials, sulcatas often spend long periods of time trying to walk or tunnel through the invisible barrier. If allowed to continue, this behavior can lead to injuries.

For outdoor tortoise maintenance, you need to build a walled-off "pen". You can make the walls out of water-sealed wood, plastic panels, cinder blocks or poured cement walls – just be sure that whatever you use has the structural stability to contend with your 200-pound battering ram of a pet.

The walls of the enclosure must extend underground for at least 12 inches (30 centimeters), to reduce the chances of the tortoises tunneling under the wall. Some keepers also find it helpful to bury wooden panels or cement around the inside perimeter of the fence, which will also help to reduce the chances of a jailbreak.

Always be sure that the interior of the enclosure is free of exposed nails, screws and other items that may harm your pet.

Layout and Size

In most cases, rectangular cage designs are superior to square or round cage designs. This is because the rectangular layout allows you to create a more effective thermal gradient in a given amount of space than a square or round layout does. Additionally, rectangular enclosures provide a longer distance that the animal can travel before reaching a barrier, which is likely to promote better health and well-being.

Nevertheless, some keepers have had great success with cages of all shapes and configurations. As long as the turtle's needs are met, any configuration will work. To some extent, you will have to customize the enclosure to suit your home or yard, given its scale.

If you are utilizing an outdoor enclosure, try to construct it in such a way that part of the enclosure receives direct sunlight, while the other portion of the enclosure lies in the shade. The grade should be relatively flat, but a slight incline is nothing to worry about, as long as your pet appears to use all areas of the cage without trouble.

Sulcata enclosures should have a large footprint, but they need not be very tall – walls that rise about 3 feet above the ground are sufficient for even the largest individuals.

The proper size for a sulcata cage or enclosure is a subject of great debate. Many authorities present conflicting suggestions. In all cases, suggested cage sizes should be considered the minimum acceptable. Larger cages are always better.

A commonly referenced guideline states that enclosures need only be five times the turtle's length long, three times the turtle's length wide, and at least two times the turtle's length in height. "Length" in these contexts refers to the length of the turtle's shell when measured in a straight line.

In other words, by this guideline, a 12-inch-long sulcata requires a 60-inch-long, 36-inch-wide, 24-inch tall enclosure.

Likewise, a 2-inch-long sulcata requires a cage 10-inches-long, 6-inches-wide and 4-inches tall.

The Zoological Association of America requires terrestrial turtles to have enclosures with an area equal to at least 10 times the area of their shell.

Therefore, if your sulcata's shell is 12 inches (30 centimeters) by 10 inches (25 centimeters), the entire enclosure must be at least 1200 square inches in size (3050 square centimeters).

However, both of these recommendations still seem quite cramped for animals that may roam about a territory measured in square miles (kilometers) in the wild.

Accordingly, many keepers (including the author) encourage sulcata owners to provide *much* more room than these recommendations. It is the author's view that sulcatas should be provided with areas that are an order of magnitude larger than the aforementioned recommendations.

This is not a critically important factor for the first few years of a sulcata's life – a 50- to 100-gallon tub or pond liner will comfortably house your pet until he is large enough to move outdoors. However, ample space is very important for the next several decades of your pet's life.

For adult sulcatas, this means cages with at least 100 square feet of space - preferably, two or three times this much. Such spacious enclosures allow the animals to obtain much more exercise than those kept in confined quarters.

In addition to the outdoor pen, your tortoises will also need a structure into which they can retreat at night or during inclement weather.

The structure can be purchased commercially or you can make it yourself. Prefabricated barns and storage sheds work well and provide the best option. Some keepers utilize doghouses or similar items, but it is important to ensure the structure is anchored securely, to prevent your pet from moving or toppling it.

If the winters in your area are too cold for outdoor activity, you will need to confine the turtles to this structure and provide supplemental heat sources. This may also be necessary at night if your area experiences low evening temperatures.

Bare earth floors are preferable to concrete. The former allow your turtle to "dig in" for the night, while the latter not only prevent digging, but they also require frequent cleaning. You can cover the soil with dried hay if you wish, but be sure to replace it if it becomes soiled.

When constructing the outdoor enclosure, it rarely makes sense to build it any smaller than will ultimately become necessary. In other words, do not make an outdoor enclosure spacious enough for your 10-inch-long sulcata; make it spacious enough to accommodate your pet once he reaches his full size.

Substrate and Furniture

Now that you have decided what type of enclosure is right for you and your tortoise, you can start placing the necessary items in the tank.

Substrates

In the wild, sulcatas live in areas with sand- and rock-based substrates. You can try to recreate this in your tortoise's captive environment by using a combination of sand and dirt.

For outdoor maintenance, bare dirt or dirt that is covered by grass or clover makes the best substrate. The substrate should be fairly dry to prevent fungi and bacteria from colonizing the enclosure and to avoid causing health problems for your pet. Most types of dirt – from rich loam to red clay – make acceptable substrates, although some will allow your pet to create tunnels better than others will.

Some keepers prefer to cover the ground with timothy or alfalfa hay, while others cover the ground with wood chips. Edible grasses and hays make suitable substrates, and serve as an additional source of forage, which can be helpful for turtle maintenance. However, wood chips represent a potential ingestion hazard, so keepers are encouraged to think carefully before using them for a substrate. If you do choose to use wood chips as a ground cover, you must avoid cedar-based products, as they are toxic to reptiles.

For indoor tortoise maintenance, dirt-sand mixtures are ideal, but you can also use hardwood mulch products, edible hays or alfalfa pellets.

Furniture

Most reptiles feel more secure in complex habitats than they do barren boxes with no visual barriers or items to investigate. Sulcatas are no exception in this regard. Place a sulcata in a cage with no furniture, and he will normally crawl head first into one of the corners.

Sulcatas usually sleep in sheltered locations.

However, you must strike a delicate balance between adding enough items to the enclosure to give your pet a sense of security and overcrowding the habitat, which makes maintenance more difficult and reduces the space available to your pet.

There are no widely accepted guidelines governing these types of decisions; you must simply experiment until you get the right proportion of furniture to open space. However, when in doubt, it is wise to err on the side of too much open space, rather than too much furniture.

Sulcatas do not need climbing branches or elevated basking platforms, as many other captive reptiles do; they need plenty of hiding places and visual barriers.

Things like large rocks, inverted plastic containers and hollow logs make good choices, just be sure that they are completely stable, and will not topple as your tortoise tromps all over them. Additionally, monitor your pets to ensure they do not begin digging under items in such a way that could make them fall or collapse.

Providing your sulcata with numerous hiding places may help prevent your pet from excavating large portions of the habitat. Additionally, it provides security to smaller individuals, who may not yet have the strength to fashion their own tunnel.

Plants

Live plants can be valuable components of a high-quality tortoise habitat, but they are not strictly necessary. You must be sure to avoid toxic plants, as your tortoise will likely try to eat most of them.

However, determining which plants are toxic to tortoises is not easy. Most of the information available has been extrapolated from data concerning dogs, cats, horses and other mammals – not tortoises. Moreover, many authorities list conflicting information.

The best approach is to utilize plants known to be safe for tortoise consumption, but always consult with your veterinarian before placing any plant species in your tortoise's habitat to be safe.

For example, the numerous varieties of *Brassica oleracea* (kale, broccoli, cauliflower, etc.) are safe, although they do not make good staple foods. Small mulberries (*Morus* spp.) and hibiscus plants (*Hibiscus* spp.) are also safe to grow in your pet's cage.

Most common lawn grasses are likely safe for tortoise consumption, but stick to varieties that are known to be safe, such as Bermuda (*Cynodon dactylon*), meadow fescue (*Festuca pratensis*) and perennial ryegrass (*Lolium perenne*).

Edible succulents, such as prickly pear cactus (*Opuntia* spp.) and aloe (*Aloe vera*), are also worthy additions to your tortoise's enclosure, which will provide both hiding opportunities and a food source.

Always avoid using artificial plants in tortoise cages, as they may choke your animal or cause damage to the turtle's digestive system.

Chapter 7: Heating and Lighting the Enclosure

Ectothermic– or "cold-blooded"– animals primarily heat their bodies via external sources, such as by basking in the sunlight or sitting on a warm rock.

When they cannot reach suitable temperatures, they cannot digest their food effectively, move as quickly as necessary or perform other behaviors and bodily functions.

This can lead the animal to become dormant, such as occurs during the winter; or, it can cause the animal to become ill. Therefore, to maintain any ectothermic animal, such as a sulcata tortoise, you must provide an enclosure with suitable temperatures.

Sulcatas are well adapted for hot, dry habitats.

Depending upon your local climate and the manner in which you house your tortoise, you may need one or more heating devices as well as the necessary monitoring equipment. Additionally, you must arrange the heating equipment in such a way that you provide the captive with a range of temperatures.

Ideal Climate for Sulcatas

Temperatures in the Sahel are generally high during the day and somewhat cooler at night. During the hottest part of the year (April through June), *average* temperatures in parts of the Sahel reach approximately 95 degrees Fahrenheit (35 degrees Celsius), and the daily highs reach 107 Fahrenheit (42 degrees Celsius) or more.

However, during the cooler portion of the year (January), average temperatures in some parts of the Sahel drop to the high 60s or low 70s Fahrenheit (20 to 25 degrees Celsius).

Overnight, the temperatures drop to between 57 and 66 degrees Fahrenheit (14 to 19 degrees Celsius), depending on the time of year.

However, while sulcatas live in areas subject to these temperature extremes, they usually avoid the highest highs and lowest lows by utilizing their burrows. Their burrows remain substantially cooler than the ambient air temperatures during the hot portion of the day and slightly warmer than the ambient temperatures during the coolest part of the night.

In light of this, it is wise to provide your sulcata with temperatures between about 65 (at night) and 90 degrees Fahrenheit (at the warm side of the enclosure, during the day).

Thermal Gradients

One of the most basic principles of animal husbandry is to provide captives with a range of conditions, from which they can choose which is the most comfortable.

For example, it is wise to provide all captives – particularly reptiles and other ectothermic critters, who modify their temperature behaviorally – with a range of temperatures in their enclosure.

Keepers call this practice establishing a *thermal gradient*. Creating a thermal gradient is fairly simple -- you just need to place the enclosure heat source(s) at one end of the cage. This way, temperatures will gradually fall with increasing distance from the heat source.

The area closest to the heat source essentially becomes a basking spot, while the far end of the cage serves as a cool retreat – intermediate temperatures allow your animal to fine-tune its internal temperature.

However, the temperatures of the enclosure need not be maintained in exactly this fashion; rather than a linear variation in temperatures, you can provide the tortoise with several "zones" of different temperatures. This will also allow your pet to move about the enclosure and regulate his temperature. Indeed, neat, linear gradients are not always feasible when maintaining tortoises outdoors. You cannot move the sun, so you are limited to shading portions of the habitat to establish a range of temperatures.

Heating Devices

You can use any of several different types of heating devices. All have different pros and cons, which make a given device work in one scenario but not another.

CAUTION: Always use care when arranging and operating heating devices and follow all of the manufacturer's instructions.

It is generally ill advised to place heating devices outdoors, but they can be added to your tortoise's shelter to keep the nighttime temperatures from falling too low.

The Sun

If you plan to keep your sulcata outdoors, the sun will serve as your primary heating source. While the sun offers many benefits to both the keeper and the kept, it also provides unique challenges.

On the plus side, the sun provides the best spectrum of light possible for tortoise maintenance, it is free and it requires no maintenance; but on the other hand, you have no control over this heat source.

At best, you can try to maximize the sun exposure of the enclosure by laying it out so that it catches the most hours of sunlight possible. You will still need to contend with overcast or rainy days, but, provided that these are not common, the occasional cool, dreary day will cause the turtles no harm.

Heat Lamps

Heat lamps are the most common type of heating device used by turtle and tortoise keepers to provide basking spots. Given the benefits of heat lamps, this makes good sense.

When reptile keepers refer to a "heat lamp", they mean a portable light socket surrounded by a shroud. A variety of different bulbs can be screwed into the receptacle. For example, some keepers prefer to use regular, incandescent light bulbs, while others prefer mercury vapor bulbs.

It is easy to adjust the temperature underneath a heat lamp by either changing the distance between the light and the substrate or swapping out the bulb for a different wattage.

Ceramic Heat Emitters

Ceramic heat emitters are used in place of a light bulb in a heat lamp fixture. However, unlike a light bulb, ceramic heat emitters produce no light. They only produce heat, which emanates from the ceramic.

On the plus side, most manufacturers claim that ceramic heat emitters are much more efficient than light bulbs. Additionally, as they produce no light, they can be used to heat the enclosure at night, without disturbing your pet's circadian rhythms.

However, ceramic heat emitters also have negative characteristics. Because they produce no light, you cannot tell if it is on or not by looking at it. This can lead to injuries if you accidentally touch it while it is on.

Ceramic heat emitters are also rather expensive, although when the efficiency and lifespan of the device is taken into consideration, this difference may become insignificant.

Heat Tape

Heat tape is plastic-covered electrical wire that is designed to heat up when current is applied. Heat tape is not appropriate for creating a basking spot, but it may help to keep indoor enclosures at the desired level, when placed underneath the habitat. However, you must be sure to allow air to flow across the heat tape to prevent a dangerous buildup of heat.

Heat tape is largely inappropriate for beginning reptile keepers, as it must be wired by hand. You must use heat tape with a thermostat or rheostat to maintain the proper temperatures. If you do not, the heat tape will become much too hot and may cause a fire.

Care must be used when laying out heat tape, as improper placement can represent a fire hazard – always follow the manufacturer's instructions when assembling or using heat tape.

Heat Pads

Heating pads made for reptiles are generally constructed by enclosing a length of pre-wired heat tape in a plastic cover. Like heat tape, heat pads are not helpful for maintaining a basking spot, but they may help heat the substrate if placed below the cage. Be sure that the manufacturer's instructions permit this type of use before using a heat pad in this manner.

Heating pads should always be used with a thermostat or rheostat to maintain appropriate temperatures.

Heat Cables

Heat cables are long conducting wires that heat up when current is applied to them. Most heat cables are covered in plastic, which may or may not make them suitable for use outdoors or in situations in which they become damp.

Like heat tape or heating pads, you must use heat cables with a rheostat or, preferably, a thermostat.

Radiant Heat Panels

Radiant heat panels are similar to heating pads, except that they are designed to project heat rather than warm things that are in contact with the device. Additionally, radiant heat panels are usually placed on the ceiling or wall of an enclosure. This makes them very helpful for providing a basking spot.

Radiant heat panels often cost more than heat lamps do, but they provide safer, more controlled heat. However, radiant heat panels must be used with a thermostat to ensure they do not overheat.

Heated Rocks and Other Items

Heated rocks, branches, caves and other items were some of the earliest and most popular commercial heating devices for pet reptiles. They are made from a faux rock (or stick, etc.) and an internal heating element.

In previous decades, heated rocks garnered a bad reputation for burning reptiles. In some cases, this was due to faulty equipment, but in many others, it was due to keeper error.

These types of devices are not designed to raise the temperature of a pet reptile's habitat – they are merely designed to provide a localized basking spot. Unfortunately, many early keepers did not understand this, and so their pet reptiles wrapped tightly around these devices, while sitting in a woefully under heated cage.

Newer designs feature built-in rheostats or thermostats and are often constructed with better components. Nevertheless, they are inappropriate for turtles of any kind, and should be avoided.

Monitoring and Control Equipment

Maintaining an appropriate climate in your pet's enclosure often requires some trial and error, but this does not mean that you should blindly approach the task.

Instead, you must measure the cage temperatures, to ensure they are within the comfortable range for your pet.

Thermometers

Tortoise keepers need two different types of thermometers to monitor their pet's environment properly: one to measure the ambient air temperatures and another to measure the surface temperatures of objects in the habitat.

Several different types of thermometers are appropriate for measuring the ambient air temperature, including analog and digital varieties. Often, digital, indoor-outdoor models are the best choice, as they feature a remote sensing probe. These probes allow you to monitor the temperature in two different portions of the habitat simultaneously, such as the basking spot and the burrow.

To measure the surface temperatures in the enclosure – such as the basking spot or the top of your pet's shell while he is under the basking spot – use an infrared, non-contact thermometer. Dedicated keepers often find these tools immensely valuable; invest in a quality unit, as you are likely to end up using it quite often.

Avoid the plastic, "stick-on" variety of thermometer often sold in pet stores.

Rheostats

Rheostats are akin to "volume controls" for heating devices. They work like lamp dimmer switches, as they reduce the amount of electricity reaching the heating device. This reduction in electricity reduces the amount of heat produced by the device.

Rheostats are helpful tools as they allow you to fine-tune the amount of heat supplied by a given device. However, you must still monitor the temperatures regularly, to ensure the cage temperatures stay within the desired range.

Thermostats

Thermostats are similar to rheostats, but they automatically adjust the amount of electricity reaching the heating device, in order to maintain a pre-selected temperature. Several different types of thermostats are available commercially.

Some work by simply switching the power to the heating device on and off. Others work by continually adjusting the amount of electricity reaching the device.

The former are called on-off thermostats while the later are termed pulse-proportional thermostats. On-off thermostats are only suitable for use with heat pads, radiant heat panels or heat tape.

While you must regularly check to ensure your thermostats are working, they are very helpful for maintaining proper cage temperatures, and they largely automate climate control.

Some thermostats feature a night-drop function, which allows you to program the unit to drop the temperatures by a preselected amount each night.

Thermostat Failure

Eventually, all thermostats will fail. Whether this occurs a week after you purchase the unit or 30 years from now remains to be seen, but you must prepare for the possibility.

In a worst-case scenario, thermostat failure can lead to the death of your animals.

You can provide yourself with some protection from thermostat failure by purchasing a high-quality unit, crafted from quality components. However, even expensive thermostats can fail.

Another option is to use two thermostats, wired in series. To accomplish this, you must set the primary thermostat to the preferred temperature range for your animal. You then attach a second thermostat behind the first. Set this thermostat to a few degrees higher than the primary thermostat.

This way, when the primary thermostat fails, the secondary thermostat will allow the temperature to rise a few degrees, but will prevent the habitat from becoming dangerously warm.

Nighttime Heating

If the nighttime temperatures in your area (or your home) do not fall lower than the mid-60s, you can probably avoid providing any form of heat during the nights.

Some keepers even allow their sulcatas to experience temperatures lower than this – some even boast of finding frost on the shells of their tortoises in the morning! However, this may increase the chances of your tortoise falling ill. Young, exceptionally old and sick tortoises are most likely to fall ill from cool temperatures, so err on the side of caution with such individuals.

It is also important to remember that the temperatures in your pet's burrow will be more moderate (warmer in cool weather, cooler in hot weather) than the ambient, aboveground temperatures.

Nevertheless, sulcatas should be provided with a significant temperature drop each night, as constantly warm conditions are unnatural and potentially harmful. Among other benefits provided by diel temperature swings is that they can inhibit bacterial and fungal growth. It also allows the turtles metabolic rate slow down for a period each day, which likely provides health benefits.

Differing Thermal Requirements

Like most other types of animals, small turtles are less tolerant of temperature extremes than large turtles are. In addition, because they have greater surface-to-volume ratios than larger tortoises do, small individuals change temperatures much more quickly than their larger counterparts do.

Accordingly, it is wise to keep the maximum temperatures available to small turtles a few degrees below that provided to large individuals, and to keep the minimum temperatures a few degrees higher than those that are provided to large tortoises.

Lighting

Most turtles require very specific lighting to remain healthy. Without it, pet turtles may develop shell irregularities, lose bone mass or suffer kidney failure, among other problems.

The easiest way to solve this problem is by maintaining your tortoise outdoors. But this is not always possible, and is not ideal for young tortoises, who are vulnerable to predators. Therefore, in lieu of natural sunlight, keepers should provide pet turtles with high quality, "full-spectrum" lighting. Full spectrum lighting refers to lights that produce not only visible light, but light in the UV portion of the range.

More specifically, turtles generally require lights that produce light in both the UVA and UVB portions of the range. UVA is defined as light between 320 and 400 nanometers, while UVB is defined as light between 290 and 320 nanometers.

UVC, which has wavelengths of between 100 and 290 nanometers, is destructive to cells, and is not produced by bulbs designed for reptile cages or general illumination.

UVA wavelengths have been shown to influence the vision and behavior of reptiles, and may play a role in food recognition. UVB wavelengths have widely been shown to allow reptiles to convert inactive vitamin D to the active form (Vitamin D3).

Vitamin D3 is crucial to the metabolism of calcium. When reptiles are deficient in vitamin D3, they tend to draw calcium from their bones. This leads to soft bones, and is termed metabolic bone disease. Often, the condition proves fatal, or becomes debilitating enough to require euthanasia. Once the symptoms of metabolic bone disease present themselves, the disease is often in an advanced state.

Most full spectrum lights are fluorescent bulbs. Both conventional and compact styles are available. Minimally, you must incorporate full spectrum bulbs over the basking site, but you can place them along the entire length of the enclosure if you prefer. However, if you choose to illuminate the entire tank with full-spectrum bulbs, be sure to offer the turtle refuges, where it can avoid the light.

The amount of UVB light emanating from the bulb dissipates rapidly with increasing distance from the lamp. This means that you must place the lights relatively close to the basking reptile – a maximum of about 12 inches (30 centimeters).

Full spectrum lights lose their ability to produce UVB over time, so you must replace them regularly. Follow the manufacturer's instruction regarding replacement schedule, but most lights last between 6 and 12 months.

Plug the full-spectrum lights into a lamp timer to keep your pet's photoperiod consistent. Because of their near-equatorial distribution, sulcatas do not experience much change in day length over the course of the year. Therefore, 12 to 14 hours of full spectrum lighting is ideal.

Chapter 8: Water and Humidity

Despite hailing from arid regions, sulcatas require water to survive. Proper hydration is critical for the health of these animals, so most keepers provide fresh drinking water to their tortoises, and some even provide their tortoises with periodic baths, to further ensure they remain hydrated.

Drinking Water

Wild sulcatas obtain much of their water through the plants they consume. Similarly, captive sulcatas obtain water from their diet, but most keepers still elect to provide fresh drinking water for their pets.

The easiest way to provide them with water is via a large, flat, shallow dish. Avoid deep, narrow water containers, as they are difficult for the tortoises to access and more likely to spill. Additionally, because tortoises are not strong swimmers, it is imperative to avoid offering water in a dish deep enough to cause the turtles to drown.

Plastic plant saucers, cat litter pans and plastic storage boxes make effective water dishes for adults, while small glass saucers, storage box lids or commercial water dishes designed for small tortoises work best for young sulcatas.

Always keep the water clean to prevent your tortoise from becoming sick. Wash the water dish every day with soap and water, but be sure to rinse it thoroughly before returning it to the enclosure. It is also wise to disinfect the water dish periodically by soaking it in a mild bleach solution for 1 hour and then rinsing it well.

Some keepers prefer to offer water periodically (perhaps twice per week) rather than keeping a water dish in the cage at all times. This helps to keep the enclosure from becoming too damp, but, as long as the enclosure has adequate ventilation, a water dish will probably not increase the humidity of the enclosure too undesirable levels.

Many keepers use tap water for their tortoises, but others prefer to use bottled spring water instead. It is possible that some of the chemicals found in tap water are harmful for your pet, so consult with your veterinarian before using tap water for your pet's drinking needs.

Soaking

In addition to providing drinking water, many tortoise keepers soak their tortoises periodically in a small bit of water. This helps to ensure they remain hydrated and often helps to dislodge dirt, grime or food stuck to the bottom of their shell.

Soak your tortoise by adding a small amount of water to a plastic storage container, bucket or similar enclosure. Only add enough water to wet the bottom of the tortoise's shell – never make your tortoise swim or struggle to keep his head above the water. This equates to about ¼ to ½ inch for hatchlings, and 1 to 2 inches for large adults.

Avoid using water that is substantially warmer or cooler than your pet's body temperature. One easy way to accomplish this is by placing the soaking container (with lukewarm water already added) into your pet's enclosure for about an hour before soaking him. This way, the water will be roughly the same temperature as the ambient temperatures in the cage, which will prevent your pet from becoming chilled or burned.

A typical soaking regimen may call for you to soak your tortoise for 20 minutes, twice per week, although some keepers provide soaks more or less frequently than this. In all cases, it is important to monitor your tortoise while he is soaking to avoid accidents.

Note that your tortoise may defecate in the water. If this happens, you must change the water immediately to prevent your pet from drinking the contaminated water.

Dry your turtle off with paper towels after soaking him, which will help keep the substrate from sticking to his shell.

Obviously, it is all but impossible to soak mature sulcatas weighing 100 pounds or more – it is not easy to get a large sulcata to do anything it does not want to do! To that end, most keepers of large sulcatas simply keep a large water container in the habitat with the sulcata, and allow it to soak and drink as it wishes.

Humidity

Though sulcatas hail from dry regions, they spend a lot of time in their burrows, where the relative humidity is much higher than it is above ground.

In fact, some recent research suggests that young tortoises may begin "pyramiding" (see chapter 13) when deprived of a high-humidity retreat.

However, they will not thrive in enclosures that are kept continually humid. This may lead to skin lesions and respiratory infections. Accordingly, it is important for sulcata owners to provide their tortoises with access to both low- and high-humidity areas within their enclosure.

For large sulcatas kept outdoors, this is rarely difficult, as long as your tortoise digs his own burrow, or you provide him with a shelter of some type. A burrow will naturally stay more humid than the surrounding area will, and it is relatively simple to sprinkle some water on the substrate inside a shelter periodically, to keep the humidity high.

For small tortoises housed indoors, a better strategy is to provide a cage with a low relative humidity and add a "damp retreat" to the cage, which your pet will use as a hiding place.

You can make a damp retreat by simply placing an inverted plastic container (with a door cut into the side to provide access for the turtle) inside the cage and dampening the substrate below it.

Chapter 9: Diet

Diet is one of the most challenging and important aspects of sulcata maintenance. Many new keepers are shocked to learn that these animals require more that lettuce scraps to stay healthy. Good health requires a diet that mimics their natural diet.

Sulcatas are grazing animals, who subsist on a broad selection of plant species in the wild. However, instead of fleshy fruits, berries and root vegetables, grasses, weeds and flowers form the bulk of the sulcata diet. As you may expect, such items are not often available at your local grocery store.

Instead, sulcata owners must be creative and use a variety of approaches for feeding their animals. Some foods can be grown in a vegetable garden, while others will grow well in your tortoise's enclosure; a few can be found at the local grocer, and yet, a few more can be found at specialty farmer's markets.

Generally, the best practice is to provide constant access to "forage" foods, on which your tortoise can feed as he wishes, and supplement this with periodic feedings that include suitable vegetables.

Food Selection

Good dietary items for sulcatas have a high fiber content and very little water and sugars.

Therefore, grasses, tree leaves and weeds should make up the bulk (75 to 80 percent) of your sulcata's diet. Most will graze on dandelions, crabgrass and fescue grown in their enclosure, but it is important to offer as many different types of these plants as possible.

Some edible grasses and weeds include:

- Barnyard grass
- Buffalo grass
- Tall fescue
- Blue fescue
- Pampasgrass
- Rye grass
- St. Augustine grass
- Sesame grass
- Oatgrass
- Timothy hay
- Alfalfa hay
- Clover
- Dandelion
- Field mustard

Banana leaves, hibiscus leaves and horseradish leaves are also valuable dietary items that you can feed to your pet. Additionally, you can provide your tortoise with leaves from edible woody plants, such as blackberry shrubs, grape vines and mulberry trees. However, you must always be sure to positively identify any plant or vegetable before giving it to your pet.

Sulcatas also relish the pads of many cacti, such as prickly pear (*Opuntia* spp.). Although it is probably wise to remove the spines before giving the pads to your pet, some keepers leave the spines intact without suffering any problems.

Dark leafy green vegetables can make up about 10 to 15 percent of your tortoise's diet. However, try to offer leafy greens that have a high calcium to phosphorus ratio, such as collard and turnip greens, rather than lettuces. Additionally, avoid feeding your pet vegetables that are high in oxalates, such as spinach and Swiss chard.

Flowers, such as those from hibiscuses, roses and nasturtiums, are relished by sulcatas, but they should only compromise 5 to 10 percent of the diet.

Avoid feeding fruits such as strawberries, tomatoes or watermelon, as the high water and sugar content of these foods can cause digestive upset for your pet. Never provide animal protein or carbohydrate-based foods (such as rodent chow, etc.) to your tortoise.

Your tortoise's feces will provide some feedback about the diet that you are providing. Healthy sulcata stools are full of long, fibrous material and are relatively dry. By contrast, sulcatas fed too much wet or nutrient-dense food produce watery, soft feces.

Realize that sulcatas will greedily eat many foods that are not healthy for them. This makes sense for wild sulcatas, who must work hard for the food they consume. The small amount of excess calories, sugar and water do not represent a problem in such instances. However, captive sulcatas, who travel less and eat more than their wild counterparts, can quickly become ill from eating too many of these types of foods. You cannot blame your sulcata for wanting delicious "treats"; but you must exercise discipline for your pet, to ensure his continued health.

A variety of commercially produced tortoise foods are on the market. While these should never make up the bulk of your tortoise's diet, many such products are probably acceptable if provided infrequently and in very small quantities. Always scrutinize the product packaging, and ensure that the food does not include any animal protein before offering it to your tortoise.

Feeding Frequency and Quantity

In addition to feeding your tortoise a diverse selection of healthy foods, you must feed your tortoise the correct amount of food to ensure good health.

As long as you provide plenty of room for exercise, avoid giving animal protein sources to your pet, provide foods that are similar to those he would eat in the wild – primarily composed of low-water, high-fiber grasses, weeds and flowers – you are unlikely to overfeed your pet. Grasses and similar foods are relatively nutrient- and calorie-poor, which means that sulcatas can eat their fill of suitable foods without becoming overweight.

In practice, keepers often accomplish this by providing their tortoise with some type of forage that is always available, and supplementing this with meals several times per week. Suitable forages include live grasses and weeds grown in the enclosure, or cut hay that is scattered in the enclosure (some keepers even use edible substrates, such as hay or alfalfa pellets). Supplemental meals should include dark leafy greens and flowers.

In general, young tortoises must eat more often than mature tortoises. Therefore, while you should provide your hatchling with four or five supplemental meals per week, your adult tortoise only requires one or two supplemental meals per weak. A good practice is to provide your tortoise with enough food that he is unable to consume all of it before he stops eating. Always remove any uneaten food promptly to avoid attracting rodents and prevent your tortoise from eating spoiled food.

Track your tortoise's growth to help ensure he receives enough food. Young tortoises should grow at a slow, yet consistent rate, while adults may eventually cease growing, they should maintain their body weight.

Preparing Food for Your Tortoise

While a little dirt is unlikely to sicken your tortoise, it makes sense to keep their food as clean as possible. Bacteria, fungi and parasites likely litter the ground of your pet's enclosure, so use a clean food dish or flat rock for your pet's supplemental meals.

Obviously, your tortoise will still be eating many things off the enclosure floor (such as live grass or bales of hale, placed in the habitat), so make every effort to keep the pen tidy.

Some keepers prepare "feeding trays" for their pets, which help to keep your pet from eating off the ground. To do so, fill several small, shallow trays with sterilized, organic potting soil. Then plant edible grass and plant seeds in the soil; after sprouting, place the tray in with your tortoise, who can then feed on the tender, young plants. You will need to make several such trays and rotate them regularly if this is to be an important food source.

While it is not strictly necessary to do so, most keepers cut or shred foods for small tortoises to make it easier for them to eat. However, this is more important for some foods than it is for others. For example, even the smallest hatchlings can handle live grasses, hibiscus leaves and flowers, but coarse vines and hay are difficult for small tortoises to handle.

Partially because of the coarse texture, young sulcatas rarely show interest in hay. However, it is important to encourage good long-term eating habits and accelerate the inclusion of hay in the diet. To do so, begin mixing in small quantities of hay in with your pet's supplemental meals while he is still young. Cut the hay into very small pieces to help the little turtle handle the food.

Vitamin and Mineral Supplementation

Many keepers supplement their sulcata's diet with vitamin and mineral powders. Presumably, this type of dietary supplementation helps to offset deficiencies caused by an improper diet. Alternatively, other keepers place cuttlebones in their pet's enclosure (which many sulcatas appear to enjoy) to provide additional calcium for the tortoise.

However, as these approaches are not without risk, it is preferable to avoid this necessity, by providing your pet with a nutritionally balanced diet that mimics their natural diet.

The problems inherent to supplements include the difficulties involved in providing a correct dosage, uncertainty over the correct levels of supplementation necessary and potential problems with palatability – some tortoises may not consume foods that have been supplemented.

Many vitamins and minerals are toxic in excessive quantities, and, veterinarians have yet to establish clear dosages and guidelines. In fact, these dietary needs surely vary with age; for example, young tortoises and egg-laying females undoubtedly require more calcium in their diet than mature males do. Failing to take these considerations into account can lead to health problems for your tortoise.

In light of these facts, it becomes apparent that the best strategy for sulcata maintenance is to provide a diet that mimics their natural diet as closely as is possible and includes plenty of variety, which will likely reduce the chances of vitamin or mineral deficiencies. Then, discuss the potential need for supplementation with your veterinarian and follow his or her advice.

A diet primarily composed of wild plants and grasses will help keep your sulcata healthy.

Chapter 10: Monitoring and Maintenance

Once you have set up your turtle's home, you must work to keep it habitable for your pet. Most illnesses in captive reptiles spring from inappropriate husbandry (particularly the failure to keep the habitat suitably clean), so be vigilant about maintaining the habitat to avoid such problems.

Cleaning Techniques and Supplies
Some of the things you may need to maintain the habitat include:

- Paper towels
- Soap-free scrub pads
- Heavy-duty, plastic bristled scrub brush
- Wire scrub brush
- Bleach
- Measuring cups
- Spray bottles
- Long-handled scrubbing tool

Maintenance Schedule
Try to establish a regular maintenance routine. Some tasks are necessary on a daily basis, while other tasks can be performed less frequently.

Daily

- Visually inspect the habitat and turtle, looking for any problems with the habitat or health concerns.
- Be sure that the habitat remains secure and that your pet cannot escape.
- Ensure that the temperatures in the habitat are within the appropriate range.

- Clean the habitat, removing any feces, urates, uneaten food or other such items from the enclosure.
- Empty, clean and refill the water dish.

Weekly

- Inspect outdoor habitats to be sure that no noxious or toxic plants have sprouted in or near the enclosure.
- Check for signs of pests, such as rodents, ants or roaches.
- Inspect any burrows or hiding spots in the cage to ensure they remain clean and safe.

Monthly

- Break down indoor habitats completely, replacing the substrate and cleaning all interior cage surfaces.
- Replace plants or cage furniture as necessary.
- Weigh and measure your turtle. This is particularly important with young turtles, so that you can monitor their growth. If your turtle is mature, and healthy, you can weigh and measure it less frequently.

Annually

- Change full-spectrum bulbs in indoor cages (some bulbs require replacement every 6 months – consult the manufacturer's instructions).
- Inspect all of the electrical cords, light fixtures and all other equipment for signs of wear.

Records
Proper record keeping is a crucial, but often neglected, aspect of reptile husbandry. Unfortunately, too many keepers neglect this simple and important practice.

Written records allow you to note trends, anticipate problems before they occur and learn from prior mistakes. By reviewing your husbandry records with your veterinarian, you may be able to figure out why a given health problem is occurring.

You can keep records in virtually any way you like. Some prefer to use elaborate record-keeping software packages, while others prefer to take handwritten notes, as with a journal. Either of these options – or any other option that suits your needs – is acceptable. The important thing is that you keep records.

You can never record too much data, but always record the source of your new pet, the date on which you acquired the turtle, and its weight (and length if possible) at the time of acquisition.

ID Number:	44522	Genus: Species/Sub:	Centro chelys sulcata	Gender: DOB:	Unknown 9/01/14	CARD #2
6.30.15 300 grams	7.07.15 Supplemental Vegetables	7.14.15 Supplemental Vegetables	7.21.15 Roses and Leaves	7.26.15 Soak		
7.01.15 Supplemental Vegetables	7.10.15 Soak	7.16.15 Supplemental Vegetables	7.23.15 Supplemental Vegetables	7.30.15 Supplemental Vegetables		
7.04.15 Supplemental Vegetables	7.12.15 Hibiscus Flowers	7.19.15 Supplemental Vegetables	7.25.15 340 grams			

Date	Notes
6-24-15	Acquired "Darwin" the sulcata tortoise from a breeder named Mark at the in-town reptile expo. Mark explained that Darwin's scientific name is Centrochelys sulcata, but some people may still call it Geochelone sulcata. Cost was $75. Mark was not sure what sex Darwin was. He said he hatched last October, but did not know the exact date.
6-25-13	I have decided to consider Darwin a boy until he gets big enough to be sure. I purchased a 40-gallon plastic tub, thermometer and a heat lamp. I am going to use a hollow log for a hiding spot for him. I put dirt and sand in the bottom of the cage.
6-26-13	Fed Darwin some collard greens and a dandelion I found outside. He ate a lot more than I thought he would!
6-28-13	Darwin ate more collard greens, a handful of grass clippings and a rose.
7-1-13	Darwing was looking hungry, so I gave him some blueberries. But then I read that fruit is not very good for them, so I won't give him any more of them. It stinks though, because he really seemed to like them.
7-8-13	Cleaned out all of Darwin's cage. He sure is messy!

Chapter 11: Acquiring a Sulcata Tortoise

Now that you have decided to get a sulcata, and you understand the care it requires, it is time to find your pet. Modern reptile enthusiasts can acquire sulcatas from a variety of sources, each with a different set of pros and cons.

PRO TIP: It is easy to get over excited about the potential of a new pet, which can lead to hasty decisions and regret. Take your time and select the perfect sulcata for you. You will have your turtle for the next several decades; you can take a few weeks to find the ideal companion.

Pet Stores

Pet stores are a common source for many beginning turtle keepers, but they are not always the best place to purchase your new pet.

The benefits of shopping at a pet store are that they usually have all of the equipment to care for your new turtle, including cages, heating devices and food items. You will usually be able to inspect the animal up close before purchase. In some cases, you may be able to choose from more than one specimen.

Many pet stores provide health guarantees for a short period, which provides you with some recourse if your new pet turns out to be ill. However, pet stores are retail establishments, and as such, you will pay more than you will from a breeder.

The drawbacks to purchasing a turtle from a pet store relate to the amount of expertise and knowledge of the staff.

While some pet stores concentrate on reptiles and may have a staff capable of providing them with proper care, many turtles languish while living in pet stores. Pet stores do not often know the pedigree of the animals they sell, nor are they likely to know the turtle's date of birth, or other pertinent information.

It is also worth considering the increased exposure to pathogens that pet store animals endure, given the constant flow of animals through the facility.

Reptile Expos

Reptile expos *can be* excellent places to acquire new animals. Reptile expos often feature resellers, breeders and retailers in the same room, all selling various types of turtles and other reptiles.

Often, the prices at such events are quite reasonable and you are often able to select from many different turtles. However, reptile expos are not without their problems.

For example, if you have a problem with your new pet, it may be difficult to find the seller after the event is over. Do not assume that a given vendor is skilled and reputable just because they have paid for a table at the event. Use your critical thinking skills and research the vendor as much as possible (you can likely do an internet search from your phone while you are speaking with him or her), before making the purchase.

Breeders

Breeders are the best place for most novices to shop for turtles. Breeders generally offer unparalleled information and support after the sale. Additionally, breeders often know the species well, and are better able to help you learn the husbandry techniques for the animal.

The disadvantage of buying from a breeder is that you must often make such purchases from a distance, either by phone or via the internet. Breeders often have the widest selection of turtles, and are often the only place to find rare forms and truly spectacular specimens.

Classified Advertisements

Newspaper and website classified advertisements sometimes include listings for turtles. While individuals, rather than businesses generally post these, they are viable options to monitor. Often, these sales include the turtle and all of the associated equipment, which is convenient for new keepers. However, be careful to avoid purchasing someone else's "problem" (i.e. a sick or maladapted turtle).

Selecting Your Turtle

Not all turtles are created equally – you want to be careful in selecting the best specimen you can find. While you can consider color or other aesthetic qualities in your selection process, they should be minor concerns. Only select turtles that appear healthy.

Health Checklist

Never purchase a sulcata displaying any of the following signs or symptoms:

- Lumps, swellings or ulcers
- Puffy or closed eyes
- Shell deformations or wounds
- Limb or tail deformations
- Overgrown beak
- Discharge from the eyes

- Discharge from the nostrils or mouth
- Discharge from the vent

If possible, observe the turtle walking on the ground. Healthy sulcatas should move easily, and be alert and active. If the turtle is small enough to be held, it should feel heavy for its size; sick turtles often feel very light.

The Gender

Whenever possible, select male sulcatas for pets. While it is true that males grow to larger sizes than females do, which is not always ideal, males do not present any of the reproductive-related challenges females do.

Female turtles – even those who are not housed with males – may produce eggs. If they cannot find a suitable egg deposition site, they may become egg bound. This can necessitate expensive and invasive surgeries, or lead to death.

The Age

Most sulcatas offered for sale in the reptile hobby are hatchling or year-old animals. However, adults appear on the market from time to time. Usually, it is wise to acquire sulcatas that are young and small; however, yearlings may be preferable for new keepers, as they are better equipped to endure keeper errors.

Chapter 12: Interacting with Your Sulcata Tortoise

You must be sure that your interactions with your turtle are safe and positive for all parties involved. Contact with a large predator (such as yourself) may cause the turtle stress, which can lead to illness and maladaptation. Additionally, improper handling can cause your pet to suffer injuries.

In general, this means that you should avoid most unnecessary physical contact with your pet. However, you need to observe your turtle for signs of illness regularly, and this will occasionally necessitate directly handling or manipulating the animal.

While it is relatively easy to handle a small sulcata, handling a large adult is a difficult task. Not only are large sulcatas heavy, they may wiggle about while you are holding them, potentially causing you to drop your tortoise. Even falls from only a few inches off the ground can cause serious injuries, so you must use great care when lifting your pet.

Handling Your Tortoise

Different techniques are necessary for handling sulcatas of different sizes. Hatchlings are relatively easy to hold, but large adults require entirely different techniques.

Suspending a turtle by its tail can lead to spinal injuries; never use a turtle's tail to support its bodyweight, regardless of its size.

Holding Small Sulcatas

The best way to hold these very small turtles is by placing your index finger on top of the animal's carapace and placing your thumb under its plastron. Do not pinch the shell too firmly, as young turtle shells lack the rigidity of adult shells.

Holding Medium-Sized Turtles

Medium-sized sulcatas require two hands to keep their body supported. Place the thumb of each hand on top of the turtle's carapace, and place the remaining fingers on the turtle's plastron, between the front and back legs.

Holding Large Sulcatas

Weighing perhaps 100 pounds or more, large sulcatas are very difficult to lift and hold. Even if you are a weightlifter capable of easily lifting this much weight, it is much more difficult to lift a 100-pound sulcata than it is 100 pound barbell. After all, barbells do not squirm or kick when they are lifted, but sulcatas do.

Accordingly, lifting a large sulcata almost always requires multiple people. To lift the immense beast, each participant should grip the bottom of the turtle's shell and lift slowly, at the same time.

Use care when lowering the tortoise back to the ground. This will help prevent injuries to both the turtle and the handlers (in the form of squished fingers or toes).

Transporting Your Sulcata

From time to time, it will be necessary to transport your pet. When doing so, you must keep the turtle protected from injury, within the appropriate temperature range and protected from sources of stress.

The best way to do so is by placing your turtle in a large plastic storage box, filled with a soft layer of newspaper or hay. Opaque boxes will keep your turtle calmer, while transparent boxes will allow you to observe the animal without opening the lid.

Be sure to drill a few ventilation holes on each of the container's vertical sides so that your pet can breathe easily. When drilling the holes, drill from the inside of the tub toward the outside, to prevent any sharp edges from contacting your turtle.

Hygiene

Turtles often carry various strains of *Salmonella* bacteria, as well as other harmful pathogens. While these bacteria rarely cause illness in the turtles, they can make humans – particularly those with compromised immune systems – very ill. In tragic cases, death can result from such infections.

Accordingly, it is imperative to employ sound hygiene practices when caring for a pet turtle. In general, this means:

- Always wash your hands with soap and warm water following any contact with your pet, the enclosure or items that have contacted either.
- Never wash turtle cages, furniture or tools in sinks or bathtubs used by humans.
- Never perform any husbandry tasks in kitchens or bathrooms used by humans.
- Keep high-risk individuals, such as those who are less than 5 years of age, elderly, pregnant or

otherwise immunocompromised, away from captive turtles and their habitats.

Chapter 13: Sulcata Tortoise Health

Like many other tortoises, sulcatas are remarkably hardy animals, who often remain healthy despite their keeper's mistakes. In fact, most illnesses that befall pet sulcatas result from improper husbandry, and are therefore, entirely avoidable.

Nevertheless, like most other reptiles, sulcatas often fail to exhibit any symptoms that they are sick until they have reached an advanced state of illness. This means that prompt action is necessary at the first hint of a problem. Doing so provides your pet with the greatest chance of recovery.

While proper husbandry is solely in the domain of the keeper, and some minor injuries or illnesses can be treated at home, veterinary care is necessary for many health problems.

Finding a Suitable Vet

While any veterinarian – even one who specializes in dogs and cats – may be able to help you keep your pet happy, it is wise to find a veterinarian who specializes in treating reptiles. Such veterinarians are more likely to be familiar with your pet species and be familiar with the most current treatment standards for reptiles.

Some of the best places to begin your search for a reptile-oriented veterinarian include:

- Veterinary associations
- Local pet stores
- Local colleges and universities

It is always wise to develop a relationship with a qualified veterinarian before you need his or her services. This way, you will already know where to go in the event of an emergency, and your veterinarian will have developed some familiarity with your pet.

When to See the Vet

Most conscientious keepers will not hesitate to seek veterinary attention on behalf of their pet. However, veterinary care can be expensive for the keeper and stressful for the kept, so unnecessary visits are best avoided.

If you are in doubt, call or email your veterinarian and explain the problem. He or she can then advise you if the problem requires an office visit or not.

However, you must always seek prompt veterinary care if your pet exhibits any of the following signs or symptoms:

- Traumatic injuries, such as lacerations, burns, broken bones, cracked shells or puncture wounds
- Sores, ulcers, lumps or other deformations of the skin
- Intestinal disturbances that do not resolve within 48 hours
- Drastic change in behavior
- Inability to deposit eggs

Remember that reptiles are perfectly capable of feeling pain and suffering, so apply the golden rule: If you would appreciate medical care for an injury or illness, it is likely that your pet does as well.

Common Health Problems

The following are some of the most common health problems that afflict sulcatas. Be alert for any signs of the following maladies, and take steps to remedy the problem.

Respiratory Infections

Respiratory infections are some of the most common illnesses that afflict turtles and other captive reptiles.

The most common symptoms of respiratory infections are discharges from the nose or mouth; however, lethargy, inappetence and behavioral changes (such as basking more often than normal) may also accompany respiratory infections.

Myriad causes can lead to this type of illness, including communicable pathogens, as well as, ubiquitous, yet normally harmless, pathogens, which opportunistically infect stressed animals.

Your turtle may be able to fight off these infections without veterinary assistance, but it is wise to solicit your vet's opinion at the first sign of illness. Some respiratory infections can prove fatal and require immediate attention.

Your vet will likely obtain samples, send of the samples for laboratory testing and then interpret the results. Antibiotics or other medications may be prescribed to help your turtle recover, and your veterinarian will likely encourage you to keep the turtle's stress level low, and ensure his enclosure temperatures are ideal.

In fact, it is usually a good idea to raise the temperature of the basking spot upon first suspecting that your turtle is suffering from a respiratory infection. Elevated body temperatures (such as those that occur when mammals have fevers) help the turtle's body to fight the infection, and many will bask for longer than normal when ill.

Metabolic Bone Disease

Metabolic bone disease (MBD) is a complicated phenomenon that befalls turtles who are provided with insufficient calcium or insufficient amounts of the active form of vitamin D (D3), which is necessary for calcium utilization.

A well-rounded, diverse diet with plenty of grasses and weeds helps to ensure your pet receives enough calcium. Additionally, many keepers supplement their turtle's food items with calcium powders. However, it is important to consult with your veterinarian to devise a suitable supplementation schedule, as providing too much calcium can be just as problematic as providing too little.

A balanced diet will provide your turtle with plenty of inactive vitamin D. To allow your pet to convert this into the active form, you must provide it with exposure to ultraviolet radiation (specifically UVB). This can be accomplished either by housing your turtle outdoors and allowing them to bask in natural sunlight, or by illuminating their enclosure with full spectrum lights that produce light in the UVB portion of the spectrum.

When deprived of proper lighting, the calcium levels in the turtle's blood fall. This causes the turtle's body to draw calcium from the bones (including the shell) to rectify the problem.

As calcium is removed from the bones, they become soft and flexible, rather than hard and rigid. This can lead to broken bones or disfigurement, which can leave your turtle unable to eat, walk or swim.

Advanced cases of MBD are rarely treatable, and euthanasia is often the only humane option. However, when caught early and treated aggressively, some of the symptoms of the disease can be stopped. Accordingly, it is of the upmost importance to seek veterinary care at the first sign of MBD.

Pyramiding

Tortoise keepers use the term "pyramiding" to refer to the improper growth and development of a tortoise's scutes. Often, each scute takes on a pyramid-like shape, being wide at the bottom, narrow at the top and significantly raised, rather than lying flat. The result is a bumpy, rather than smooth, carapace.

The condition's cause was initially thought to be related to a poor diet, rich in animal protein. While animal-based food sources are not healthy for sulcatas, research has shown that diets rich in animal products do not cause this particular malady.

Currently, most of the available evidence points to water and hydration levels as being the most important factor in causing pyramiding. It appears that chronic dehydration during the turtle's early years causes the scutes to form abnormally.

Accordingly, it is important to provide young tortoises with a humid retreat, in which they will spend considerable amounts of time. This mimics the wild lifestyle of sulcata tortoises; although they live in very dry environments, their burrows remain relatively humid, which keeps the turtles from dehydrating.

Pyramiding is permanent once it occurs, so it is of paramount importance to provide young sulcatas with the correct husbandry.

This tortoise's shell displays significant pyramiding.

Shell Rot
Shell rot is a catchall term for a variety of maladies related to a turtle's shell. Shell rot normally takes the form of lesions or ulcers; sometimes, a small amount of fluid may leak from the wounds.

Shell rot may occur because of a systematic infection or as a local phenomenon. Bacteria or fungi may be the primary cause of the problem, or injuries may provide an opportunity for pathogens to colonize the tissues.

Shell rot is usually treatable with prompt veterinary care, so always see your veterinarian at the first sign of problems.

Parasites
Parasites are rare among captive-bred sulcatas, but poor husbandry can cause them to become a problem. Parasites

rarely become problematic for wild turtles, unless they become injured, stressed or ill.

Most internal parasites cause intestinal problems, such as runny or watery stools, vomiting or decreased appetites. Your veterinarian can collect blood or stool samples from your turtle, analyze them to determine what parasites, if any, are present, and prescribe medications to clear the infestation. Often, multiple treatments are necessary to eradicate the parasites completely.

External parasites afflict sulcatas on occasion, usually in the form of ticks. Because some ticks carry dangerous diseases, you should have your veterinarian inspect any animal carrying the parasitic arthropods.

Anorexia

Sulcatas are normally ravenous eaters, who rarely pass up the chance to consume calories. However, they may refuse food if ill, if kept in suboptimal temperatures (including seasonally cool temperatures, such as occur during the winter) or are preoccupied by breeding.

Refusing a meal or two is not cause for alarm, but if your turtle refuses food for longer than this, be sure to review your husbandry practices. If the turtle continues to refuse food without an obvious reason for doing so, consult your veterinarian.

Injuries

Despite their protective shells and armored legs, sulcatas can become injured in myriad ways, including battles with cagemates, overly zealous breeding attempts, or by sustaining burns from heaters. While tortoises are likely to heal from most minor wounds without medical attention, serious wounds will necessitate veterinary assistance.

Your vet will likely clean the wound, make any repairs necessary (shell patches, sutures, etc.) and prescribe a course of antibiotics to help prevent infection. Be sure to keep the enclosure as clean as possible during the healing process.

Egg Binding

Egg binding occurs when a female is unable or unwilling to deposit her eggs in a timely fashion. If not treated promptly, death can result.

The primary symptoms of egg binding are similar to those that occur when a gravid turtle approaches parturition. Egg bound turtles may dig to create an egg chamber or attempt to escape their enclosure. However, unlike turtles who will deposit eggs normally, egg bound turtles continue to exhibit these symptoms without producing a clutch of eggs.

As long as you are expecting your turtle to lay eggs, you can easily monitor her behavior and act quickly if she experiences problems. However, if you are not anticipating a clutch, this type of problem can catch you by surprise.

Prolapse

Prolapses occur when a turtle's intestines protrude from its vent. This is an emergency situation that requires prompt treatment. Fortunately, intestinal prolapse is not terribly common among tortoises.

You will need to take the animal to the veterinarian, who will attempt to re-insert the intestinal sections. Sometimes sutures will be necessary to keep the intestines in place while the muscles regain their tone.

Try to keep the exposed tissue damp, clean and protected while traveling to the vet. It is likely that this problem is very painful for the animal, so try to keep its stress level low during the process.

Quarantine

Quarantine is the practice of isolating animals to prevent them from transferring diseases between themselves.

If you have no other pet reptiles (particularly turtles), quarantine is unnecessary. However, if you already maintain other turtles (especially other sulcatas) you must provide all new acquisitions with a separate enclosure.

At a minimum, quarantine all new acquisitions for 30 days. However, it is wiser still to extend the quarantine period for 60 to 90 days, to give yourself a better chance of discovering any illness present before exposing your colony to new, potentially sick, animals. Professional zoological institutions often quarantine animals for six months to a year. In fact, some zoos keep their animals in a state of perpetual quarantine.

Chapter 14: Breeding Sulcata Tortoises

Many – if not most – turtle keepers are eventually bitten by the captive breeding bug. Determined to produce a clutch of adorable hatchlings, these keepers acquire specimens of each sex and begin waiting for eggs.

This is a natural progression for keepers, and, when carried out in responsible fashion, breeding can be beneficial for the species, as captive breeding projects help alleviate pressure on wild populations.

However, irresponsible breeders often cause serious problems for the hobby.

Such breeders often set out with the explicit goal of profiting from their turtles, rather than enjoying their pets in their own right. This ensures failure for the vast majority of people that try to breed turtles for profit.

Pre-Breeding Considerations

Before you set out to breed sulcatas, consider the decision carefully. Unfortunately, few keepers realize the implications of breeding their turtles before they set out to do so.

Ask yourself if you will be able to:

- Provide adequate care for a pair of adult turtles
- Provide the proper care for the female while gravid
- Afford emergency veterinary services if necessary
- Incubate 30 or more eggs in some type of incubator
- Provide housing for 30 or more hatchlings
- Provide food for 30 or more hatchlings
- Dedicate the time to caring for 30 or more hatchlings

- Find new homes for 30 or more hatchlings

If you cannot answer each of these questions affirmatively, you are not in a position to breed sulcatas responsibly.

Legal Issues

Before deciding to breed tortoises, you must investigate the relevant laws in your area. Some municipalities require turtle breeders to obtain licenses, insurance and permits, although others do not.

Finally, be aware that it is illegal to buy or sell turtles with carapaces less than 4 inches in length in the United States, except for educational or scientific purposes. This is a particularly important consideration when breeding prolific turtles, such as sulcatas, because you will have to care for the offspring until for at least one year, while waiting for them to attain the minimum size necessary.

Sexing Sulcatas

If, after considering the proposition carefully, you decide to breed sulcatas, you will need at least one sexual pair of animals. To be sure that you have a sexed pair, you must be able to distinguish one sex from the other.

This can be a difficult task with young tortoises, as the differences between the two are negligible. However, by the time they reach about 12 to 14 inches in length, it becomes much easier to discern their sex.

The best way to distinguish the sex of a sulcata is by observing the plastron; it helps if you have more than one animal, thereby allowing you to compare and contrast.

The anal scutes (those on both sides of the tail) of mature males are more widely spread than those of females are.

Additionally, males have concave plastrons, while females have flat plastrons.

Pre-Breeding Conditioning

Once you have obtained a sexual pair, you must begin conditioning them for breeding. This is important because animals that are not in very good condition may not be able to handle the rigors of cycling and breeding.

Take the turtles to visit your veterinarian, who will be able to ascertain their health status. Some veterinarians may only perform a visual inspection, but others may collect biological samples for additional testing.

If your vet determines that your turtles are not healthy, take whatever steps are recommended to rectify the problem before commencing breeding trials.

Once you are certain that your turtles are in good health, it is time to initiate your breeding protocols.

Cycling

Cycling is a term used to describe the practice of providing captive reptiles with an annual variation in temperature (or other factors, such as photoperiod). The concept seeks to mimic the natural seasonal cycle and synchronize the reproductive cycle of the reptiles in question.

In some species, proper cycling appears to be necessary for successful reproduction in captivity, while other species reproduce quite successfully with no variation in temperature or any other factor. Because most sulcata keepers maintain their animals outdoors, they are already exposed to a natural seasonal cycle.

Wild sulcatas generally breed from September through November, immediately after the raining season. However, in captivity, your tortoises may establish a different seasonal pattern in response to the local climate. Captives in the United States often breed in the late summer or early fall, with females depositing eggs in December.

Groupings and Housing

Some keepers prefer to keep the sexes separate for most of the year, and only introduce them to each other during breeding trials.

One of the benefits to keeping the sexes segregated is that it often results in vigorous courting and breeding by the male. As they say, absence makes the heart grow fonder. Additionally, singular maintenance reduces the likelihood of injuries and stress for both occupants.

While keeping your sulcatas in separate enclosures may be ideal, it is rarely realistic, nor is it necessary. Few keepers can devote enough space for multiple sulcata enclosures, and males are rarely reticent to breed (in fact, the opposite problem – continued, non-stop breeding – is often the problem). Instead, most keepers maintain breeding pairs together all year long.

Male sulcatas often emit vocalizations while mating.

In fact, many keepers maintain their sulcatas in small groups. This usually works well if the enclosure is large enough and no more than one male is kept in the pen. Cohabitating males will battle viciously, which can lead to injuries, stress and domination.

Gravid

Shortly after successful copulation, suitably healthy females become gravid. Unlike many other reptiles, turtles do not offer very many signs to indicate their reproductive condition.

Manual palpation, which is a common method for determining the reproductive condition of many other reptiles, is rarely helpful with turtles. In fact, attempting to feel a female's eggs with your fingers may cause them to rupture. Accordingly, it is wise to avoid the practice entirely. Instead, the best clues lie in the female's behavior.

Many gravid sulcata females begin eating very little food as their eggs develop and take up more space in their body cavity. They may also begin to explore their surroundings and look for a suitable place to dig their eggs.

Nevertheless, the only way to be certain that your turtle is gravid is by having your veterinarian perform an x-ray. This will not only verify that she is holding eggs, but it will allow you to know approximately how many eggs she is carrying. However, given the size of sulcatas and the difficulty involved in transporting them, few keepers go to this trouble unless their tortoise shows signs of difficulty, such as being egg-bound.

Egg Deposition

As the time for egg deposition nears, the female will become increasingly restless. She may pace for long periods of time or even look for a way to escape from the enclosure.

At this point, the female is seeking out a place to dig a nest and deposit her eggs. Hopefully, you have designed the enclosure so that such a place is always available, but, if you have not, you must provide her with a place she finds suitable.

Typically, sulcatas look for a warm, sunny area, with a substrate suitable for nest construction. They prefer an area of exposed dirt, rather than having to dig through grass or vegetation.

Ideally, the egg-deposition site should have a footprint of at least two to three times the size of the turtle's shell and contain substrate as deep as the turtle's shell is long.

In other words, a 12-inch female would require an egg-deposition site that provides about 2- to 3-square-feet of space and a substrate at least 12 inches deep. In most outdoor pens, space for nesting and egg deposition is not a problem.

If your female does not find the provided site to her liking, you will need to tweak it until she feels comfortable. This can mean loosening the substrate, compacting the substrate, providing a greater depth of substrate or moving the egg deposition site to another location in the enclosure.

This is often a challenging component of turtle breeding, and even highly experienced zookeepers occasionally have problems devising a suitable egg-laying site.

If your turtle cannot find a suitable place to lay her eggs, she may scatter the eggs in the enclosure or retain them internally. Usually, these outcomes lead to health problems for the female, such as dystocia (egg binding).

Assuming that your turtle finds the egg deposition area suitable, she will eventually crawl into it, dig a small depression and fill it with eggs. After completing the process, she will cover the hole and leave the area. It can be very difficult to locate a nest site afterwards, so do your best to mark the location during, or immediately after, parturition.

Egg Incubation

Keepers employ any of several different strategies for incubating sulcata eggs. No one method is "correct," although artificially incubating the eggs in a climate-controlled container usually leads to the greatest success.

The least labor-intensive approach is to leave the eggs where they are and let them incubate naturally. After all, sulcatas have been incubating their eggs in just this way for millions of years.

However, doing so is unlikely to lead to a high rate of success, as you have little control over the temperatures of the mass. Additionally, the eggs may be vulnerable to predators, including rodents or fire ants.

You will need to be very observant for emerging hatchlings, which may make their way out of the nest over the course of a month or more. Hatchlings may be crushed by the adults very easily, so you should remove them as quickly as possible.

If you would prefer more control of the incubation process, you can excavate the egg chamber, remove the eggs and place them in a climate-controlled incubator for the remainder of their development.

Sulcata eggs are relatively robust, and tolerate a wide range of incubation temperatures; however, temperatures between 70 and 82 degrees Fahrenheit (21 to 27 degrees Celsius) lead to the best results. Temperatures outside of this range often lead to poor hatch rates.

Use great care when excavating the egg chamber to prevent damaging the eggs. Once you have accessed the eggs, mark the top of each with a graphite pencil. This will allow you to maintain the correct orientation when transferring the eggs to the incubator; inverting the eggs can cause the embryos to drown.

Avoid separating any eggs that have adhered to each other. While it is often possible to do so without damaging the eggs, such attempts should be left to those who have considerable experience incubating reptile eggs.

Egg Boxes

Egg boxes are small plastic storage boxes designed to hold the eggs inside the incubator. While their use is not always necessary in the strictest sense, they make it easier to maintain the climate surrounding the eggs.

Virtually any type of small plastic storage box will suffice, but consider a few things before selecting your egg boxes:

1. Be sure to select boxes that are tall enough to contain 1 or 2 inches (2.5 to 5 centimeters) of incubation media as well as the eggs, which will rest on top of the media (partially buried).
2. Whenever possible, select transparent egg boxes so that you can observe the eggs without having to open them.
3. If possible, select boxes with domed lids, which will help prevent condensation from dripping on the eggs.

You will need to make two small holes (approximately one-quarter-inch or one-half centimeter in diameter) in each box to allow for air exchange inside the egg boxes.

Some breeders prefer to monitor the temperature of the egg boxes, while others prefer to monitor the temperature of the incubator. Either method will work, although if you desire to measure the temperatures inside the egg boxes, you will need to drill additional holes to accept a temperature probe.

You can select relatively large egg boxes so that they will accommodate large clutches, or you can use relatively small egg boxes, so that you can split up the clutch into several different sub groups.

Incubation Media

Several different incubation media are appropriate for egg incubation. Soil, soil and sand mixtures and vermiculite are some of the most common choices by breeders. Vermiculite works for a wide variety of reptile eggs, as it is quite easy to attain a suitable moisture level.

The substrate not only provides a protective cushion that supports the eggs, but it also provides moisture, which will keep the relative humidity of the egg box high. This will prevent the eggs from desiccating.

Too much humidity or dampness, however, can have a negative effect on the eggs, so it is important to keep enough water in the egg boxes, but not too much.

Many keepers strive to maintain humidity levels of 80 percent in the egg chamber, but others simply watch the eggs and adjust the humidity accordingly. If the eggs begin to exhibit wrinkles, they are drying out and more water is necessary. Conversely, if they begin to swell or exude fluid, the humidity should be lowered.

Some authorities recommend specific ratios of water and vermiculite, but as vermiculite absorbs water from the air, it is impossible to know how saturated the vermiculite was when you started.

Accordingly, the best approach is to judge the moisture with your hands. Beginning with dry vermiculite, slowly add water while stirring the mixture. The goal is to dampen the vermiculite just enough that it clumps when compressed in your hand. However, if water drips from the media when you squeeze it, the vermiculite is too damp.

The Incubator

You can either purchase a commercially produced incubator or construct your own. However, most beginning breeders are better served by purchasing a commercial incubator than making their own.

Commercial Incubators

Commercial egg incubators come in myriad styles and sizes. Some of the most popular models are similar to those used to incubate poultry eggs (these are often available for purchase from livestock supply retailers).

These incubators are constructed from a large foam box, fitted with a heating element and thermostat. Some models feature a fan for circulating air; while helpful for maintaining a uniform thermal environment, models that lack these fans are acceptable.

You can place an incubation medium directly in the bottom of these types of incubators, although it is preferable to place the media (and eggs) inside small plastic storage boxes, which are then placed inside the incubator.

These incubators are usually affordable and easy to use, although their foam-based construction makes them less durable than most premium incubators are.

Other incubators are constructed from metal or plastic boxes; feature a clear door, an enclosed heating element and a thermostat. Some units also feature a backup thermostat, which can provide some additional protection in case the primary thermostat fails.

These types of incubators usually outperform economy, foam-based models, but they also bear higher price tags. Either style will work, but, if you plan to breed turtles for many years, premium models usually present the best option.

Homemade Incubators

Although incubators can be constructed in a variety of ways, using many different materials and designs, two basic designs are most common.

The first type of homemade incubator consists of a plastic, glass or wood box, and a simple heat source, such as a piece of heat tape or a low-wattage heat lamp. The heating source must be attached to a thermostat to keep the temperatures consistent. A thermometer is also necessary for monitoring the temperatures of the incubator.

Some keepers make these types of incubators from wood, while others prefer plastic or foam. Although glass is a poor insulator, aquariums often serve as acceptable incubators; however, you must purchase or construct a solid top to retain heat.

Place a brick on the bottom of the incubator, and place the egg box on top of the brick, so that the eggs are not resting directly on the heat tape. The brick will also provide thermal mass to the incubator, which will help maintain a more consistent temperature.

The other popular incubator design adds a quantity of water to the design to help maintain consistent temperatures and a higher humidity. To build such a unit, begin with an aquarium fitted with a glass or plastic lid.

Place a brick in the bottom of the aquarium and add about two gallons of water to the aquarium; ideally, the water level should stop right below the top of the brick.

Add an aquarium heater to the water and set the thermostat to the desired temperature. Place the egg box on the brick, insert a temperature probe into the egg box and cover the aquarium with the lid (you may need to purchase a lid designed to allow the cords to pass through it).

This type of incubator works by heating the water, which will in turn heat the air inside the incubator, which will heat the eggs. Although it can take several days of repeated adjustments to get these types of incubators set to the exact temperature you would like, they are very stable once established.

Incubation Temperature and Duration

As with the adult animals, the biological processes taking place inside reptile eggs are determined by the temperature at which they are kept. The warmer the environment is, the quicker the eggs develop; the cooler the environment is, the longer it takes the eggs to complete their development.

This basic principle holds true for sulcatas. However, this does not mean that their eggs can be incubated at any temperature. Eggs kept below the minimum acceptable temperature will fail to live, just as those kept above the maximum acceptable temperature.

The ideal range for sulcata egg incubation is between about 80 and 88 degrees Fahrenheit. Higher incubation temperatures cause the embryos to develop more quickly than those incubated at lower temperatures do.

These are relatively low temperatures relative to other reptiles, and – depending on the temperature of your home – you may be able to incubate the eggs at "room temperature."

However, doing so will invariably expose the eggs to temperature fluctuations. Minor temperature fluctuations are not harmful to the eggs, but massive swings in temperature predispose the eggs to failure or cause the young to be abnormal.

The duration of incubation varies depending on the temperature and the length of the female's gestation period. Most sulcata eggs hatch approximately 75 to 100 days after being deposited. However, individual sulcatas develop at slightly different speeds, so the young may hatch over a period of weeks. In some cases, the first and last hatchling to emerge from the eggs may be separated by a month's time.

Sex Determination

The sex of sulcatas is likely determined by the temperature at which they are incubated. This phenomenon is called temperature dependent sex determination (abbreviated TSD or TDSD) and is common among many different reptile lineages, including crocodilians, geckos and many other chelonians.

This means that, in theory, you can control the temperature of the egg mass (or individual eggs) with precision, you can deliberately create male or female hatchlings.

The problem is that the exact temperature range at which males or females are produced is not well understood. This is largely due to the difficulties involved in sexing young sulcatas (breeders would need to keep their hatchlings for several years to determine if their approach worked).

With more research and information, deliberate sex determination may become more practical.

Neonatal Husbandry

Observe the hatchlings as they emerge from their shells. Some turtles will remain in their shells for several days while they absorb the rest of their egg yolk. This is perfectly normal, and you should NOT remove such turtles from their eggs. Allow the turtle to absorb the entire yolk and exit the egg on his own.

If for some reason, the egg becomes destroyed (such as through the activities of the clutchmates), move the turtle into a clean, plastic container with about 1/4 inch of water in the bottom. Do not pull the yolk free, and try to keep it from drying out.

Once the turtles have hatched and absorbed their egg yolk, they are ready to move to the nursery. The nursery container should be constructed from a small plastic storage box (you can split the clutch among several different boxes to reduce the stress on the hatchlings).

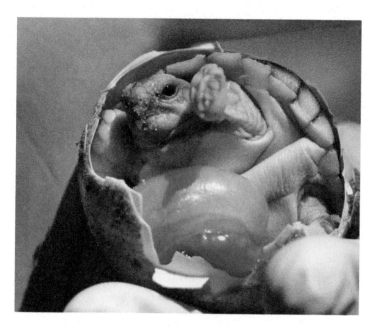

This hatchling has yet to absorb its egg yolk fully.

Drill or melt a few small ventilation holes in the top (always making sure the holes are drilled from the inside toward the outside to prevent any sharp edges from injuring the hatchlings) and place a few layers of paper towels on the bottom.

Add a very shallow water dish to the center of the cage (a 3-inch plant saucer works well) and keep it full of clean water. Leave the hatchlings inside the nursery for at least 24 hours to ensure they have absorbed their egg yolks are have become active.

Once a turtle has become active, you can move it to its "permanent" home. You can house a few hatchlings together in the same habitat, but avoid overcrowding them, which can lead to squabbles and injuries. Be sure there are more places to hide than there are turtles in the tank.

You can begin feeding them almost immediately after placing them in their new homes, but many will not begin feeding for a few days.

Chapter 15: Unusual Sulcata Tortoises

Although most sulcatas are relatively similar looking, many animals do have subtle individual differences. This is largely a byproduct of normal, individual variation, but every once in a while, a genetic mutation pops up that gives rise to animals whose unusual looks far surpass what can be explained by normal individual variation.

For example, instead of being clad in tones, some sulcatas hatch as beautiful cream or yellow animals. Often these rare individuals are quite striking, and sulcata enthusiasts prize them.

Nevertheless, because of the way in which these mutations are passed from parent to offspring, these spectacular animals remain relatively rare, even among captive populations.

An "ivory" sulcata hatchling.

Common Mutations

In contrast to some other common reptile pets, such as ball pythons (*Python regius*) and leopard geckos (*Eublepharis macularius*), for which many color mutations have been discovered, only a handful of color mutations have been documented in sulcatas.

Sometimes, the distinction between an animal harboring a genetic mutation and one that simply looks different because of individual variation is difficult to determine. Ultimately, breeding trials are necessary to determine whether the trait is a heritable condition.

At the time of this publication, several different sulcata color mutation occur in the captive gene pool, but many of the details surrounding these odd tortoises are not clear. Different breeders embrace different labels and varying criteria for those labels.

"Ivory" and albino mutations are two of the most commonly seen, but even these mutations are surrounded in confusion and sloppy terminology. Both are essentially pale-colored tortoises, whose colors are quite bright and distinctive.

Most breeders distinguish between the two mutations by noting the animals' eyes. Albinos have no pigment in their eyes, which gives them a red appearance (courtesy of the visible blood vessels in the eyes), while ivory animals retain the dark eyes characteristic of normal sulcatas. However, some keepers report that ivory sulcatas possess red eyes for a short time after hatching.

Until the nature of these mutations becomes clearer, it is wise to research any purported mutation carefully before spending thousands of dollars on a pet, and analyze the breeding history and results of the trait.

Patterns of Inheritance

It appears that most sulcata mutations are inherited in simple recessive fashion; however, it is quite possible that dominant or incomplete dominant mutations will occur in the future.

Turtles receive one copy of each gene from their mother and one from their father. Some genes affect the animal's appearance when only one copy is present, while others require two copies of a gene to express the associated trait.

Animals with two copies of the same gene are said to be homozygous. Conversely, animals with one copy of a mutant gene and one copy of the normal gene are called heterozygous.

Simple Recessive

Simple recessive traits are only expressed when an animal has two copies of the mutant gene. However, normal looking, but heterozygous animals may produce offspring that display the trait associated with the gene, if the other parent has a copy of the gene as well.

Dominant

Dominant traits are expressed whenever they are present, regardless of the other gene in the pair. Accordingly, dominant traits become very common in a given gene pool. For example, the genes associated with the normal appearance of sulcatas are dominant over most genes.

There is no visual difference between an animal with one copy of a dominant gene or two copies of the gene. However, animals that are homozygous for the dominant trait only produce young that express the dominant gene.

Incompletely Dominant

Incompletely dominant mutations are similar to dominant mutations except that those with one copy of the gene look different from those with two copies of the mutant gene.

Often, heterozygous animals display a trait (such as some forms of hypomelanism), while homozygous animals display a more extreme version of the trait (such as the so-called "super hypomelanistic" animals).

Often, incompletely dominant mutations are called co-dominant mutations. However, this terminology is not technically correct, as animals that display co-dominant traits possess more than one mutant gene.

Polygenetic Traits

Some physical traits of sulcatas are determined by the complicated interactions of several different genes. Size potential and growth rate, for example, are likely controlled by a collection of genes.

Polygenetic traits are not inherited in a predictable fashion. However, they can often be refined through selective breeding efforts.

Genetic Traits and Marketing

Unusual specimens often command very high prices, which can make turtle breeding a profitable endeavor in some cases. While there is nothing inherently wrong with this fact, the prospect of high profits often leads keepers to experience problems.

While some of these problems are born of honest mistakes or misunderstandings, others are the result of outright fraud.

To avoid these problems, those who hatch unusual looking turtles should attempt to reproduce the mutation before labelling it as a genetically inheritable condition. However, in an effort to get the animals to market quickly, some breeders market the animals in deceptive ways.

Accordingly, it is always wise to do your homework before deciding to purchase a sulcata with a rare color mutation. Additionally, it is wise to avoid purchasing turtles from shady, disreputable or evasive breeders, particularly if they are making extraordinary claims about their animals.

Chapter 16: Supplemental Information

Never stop learning more about your new pet's natural history, biology and captive care. Doing so will help you provide your new pet with the highest quality of life possible.

Further Reading

Bookstores and online book retailers often offer a treasure trove of information that will advance your quest for knowledge. While books represent an additional cost involved in reptile care, you can consider it an investment in your pet's well-being. Your local library may also carry some books about turtles, which you can borrow for no charge.

University libraries are a great place for finding old, obscure or academically oriented books about turtles. You may not be allowed to borrow these books if you are not a student, but you can view and read them at the library.

Herpetology: An Introductory Biology of Amphibians and Reptiles

By Laurie J. Vitt, Janalee P. Caldwell

Academic Press, 2013

Understanding Reptile Parasites: A Basic Manual for Herpetoculturists & Veterinarians

By Roger Klingenberg D.V.M.

Advanced Vivarium Systems, 1997

Infectious Diseases and Pathology of Reptiles: Color Atlas and Text

Elliott Jacobson

CRC Press

Designer Reptiles and Amphibians

Richard D. Bartlett, Patricia Bartlett

Barron's Educational Series

Magazines

Like books, magazines can offer an abundance of information. Additionally, because they are typically published several times each year, they often provide more current information than books do.

Reptiles Magazine

www.reptilesmagazine.com/

This publication covers all facets of reptile husbandry, breeding and care.

Practical Reptile Keeping

http://www.practicalreptilekeeping.co.uk/

Practical Reptile Keeping is a popular publication aimed at beginning and advanced hobbies. Topics include the care and maintenance of popular reptiles as well as information on wild reptiles.

Websites

With the explosion of the internet, it is easier to find information about reptiles than it has ever been. However, this growth has cause an increase in the proliferation of both good information and bad information.

While knowledgeable breeders, keepers and academics operate some websites, other webmasters lack the same dedication and scientific rigor. Anyone with a computer and internet connection can launch a website and say virtually anything they want about turtles. Accordingly, as with all other research, consider the source of the information before making any husbandry decisions.

The Reptile Report

www.thereptilereport.com/

The Reptile Report is a news-aggregating website that accumulates interesting stories and features about reptiles from around the world.

Kingsnake.com

www.kingsnake.com

Started as a small website for gray-banded kingsnake enthusiasts, Kingsnake.com has become one of the largest reptile-oriented portals in the hobby. Includes classifieds, breeder directories, message forums and other resources.

The Vivarium and Aquarium News

www.vivariumnews.com/

The online version of the former publication, The Vivarium and Aquarium News provides in-depth coverage of different reptiles and amphibians in a captive and wild context.

Journals

Journals are the primary place professional scientists turn when they need to learn about turtles. While they may not make light reading, hobbyists stand to learn a great deal from journals.

Herpetologica

www.hljournals.org/

Published by The Herpetologists' League, Herpetologica, and its companion publication, Herpetological Monographs cover all aspects of reptile and amphibian research.

Journal of Herpetology

www.ssarherps.org/

Produced by the Society for the Study of Reptiles and Amphibians, the Journal of Herpetology is a peer-reviewed publication covering a variety of reptile-related topics.

Copeia

www.asihcopeiaonline.org/

Copeia is published by the American Society of Ichthyologists and Herpetologists. A peer-reviewed journal, Copeia covers all aspects of the biology of reptiles, amphibians and fish.

Nature

www.nature.com/

Although Nature covers all aspects of the natural world, there is plenty to appeal to turtle enthusiasts.

Supplies

While you can obtain some of the supplies you need from local pet stores, home improvement stores and grocery stores, you may need to search widely to find some supplies and tools. Some of the following retailers sell a variety of husbandry tools and supplies.

Big Apple Pet Supply

http://www.bigappleherp.com

Big Apple Pet Supply carries most common husbandry equipment, including heating devices, water dishes and substrates.

LLLReptile

http://www.lllreptile.com

LLL Reptile carries a wide variety of husbandry tools, heating devices, lighting products and more.

Doctors Foster and Smith

http://www.drsfostersmith.com

Foster and Smith is a veterinarian-owned retailer that supplies husbandry-related items to pet keepers.

Support Organizations

Sometimes, the best way to learn about tortoises is to reach out to other keepers and breeders. Check out these organizations, and search for others in your geographic area.

The National Reptile & Amphibian Advisory Council

http://www.nraac.org/

The National Reptile & Amphibian Advisory Council seeks to educate the hobbyists, legislators and the public about reptile and amphibian related issues.

American Veterinary Medical Association

www.avma.org

The AVMA is a good place for Americans to turn if you are having trouble finding a suitable reptile veterinarian.

The World Veterinary Association

http://www.worldvet.org/

The World Veterinary Association is a good resource for finding suitable reptile veterinarians worldwide.

References

Anderson, S. P. (2003). The Phylogenetic Definition of Reptilia. *Systematic Biology*.

Crawford, N. G. (2012). A phylogenomic analysis of turtles. *Molecular Phylogenetics and Evolution*.

Houerou, H. L. (1980). The Rangelands of the Sahel. *Journal of Rangeland Management*.

Nicholson, S. E. (1995). *Sahel, West Africa*. Florida State University.

Ritz, J., Griebeler, E. M., Huber, R., & Clauss, M. (2010). Body size development of captive and free-ranging African spurred tortoises (Geochelone sulcata): high plasticity in reptilian growth rates. *The Herpetological Journal*.

Index

Published by IMB Publishing 2015

CPSIA information can be obtained
at www.ICGtesting.com
Printed in the USA
BVOW11s1116150617

486945BV00007B/171/P